FABRIC OF BASEBALL

PAQUITO MONTAÑEZ

COVER & TEXT LAYOUT
By the Author

Fabric of Baseball
ISBN 9780692789568

In Memorian
Coach Rich Tomoleoni

He had a grin on, and I don't know if to scold me or laugh as usual while eyeballing the Wildcats in the dugout. He assumed I could take the varsity second base slot, and he'd been trying to make me bend the knees to catch ground balls. About the only time I challenged his teachings, questioning him why I should bend my knees if I had a glove on.

While Mister Tom knew bending the knees is second nature to completing the play, he was buying time to laugh louder only on my second day trying out for the team. Upon returning his hawkish pupils over mine he sent me to third base, and it became home. He made sure to inform the team that I was the only player allowed to challenge the fundamentals, for as long as everyone laughed louder than him.

He was right on the fundamentals, and I was wrong until 20 years later Omar Vizquel proved that catching the ball gives you no time to bend nothing, just to complete the play. Bending the knees is already built in the principle of stellar fielding through grueling practice, and Mister Tom had no problem with forming good habits.

At third base and thereafter, the coach that earned 737 wins in the Chicago Public High School Baseball League laughed while asking me if I was born with a glove attached to my left hand.

"Roberto Clemente is the darling of San Juan fans just as he is among the Forbes Field faithful. His nickname—Arriba—was given him by former teammate Lino Donoso and when Pirate play-by-play broadcaster Bob Prince started to use it too, the fans picked it up. Freely translated it means 'arise, awake, more'. The fans have added 'Vamos' to the 'Arriba', which means 'let's go', and the chant begins everytime Clemente comes to bat."

~Pittsburgh Pirates 1960 Yearbook

***

"Sandor Boatly had never guessed that properly played, baseball consisted of mathematics, geometry, art, philosophy, balet, and carnival, all intertwined like the mystical ribbons of color in a rainbow."

~William Patric Kinsella
Author of Shoeless Joe and Butterfly Winter

Prologue
Reengineering or result of a magnificent obsession?

"The day my father gazed at the endless expanse of the desert, he wanted to build a baseball field. He made a mark on the ground and mumbled something about where to put the bases."

~Ken Mochizuki
Baseball saved us

W ho'll buy the idea? Why so deep in the restructure? Abruptly? Will you bark from behind the desk? Too darn deep Elmer. It was all I heard from Ruperto's highlands dialect. In his calm demeanor, he followed that any restructure must count with the influential. Must admit the apparently dynamic Millenials, and those refining their local baseball programs. Contemplating the timespan of a restructure bringing the sport to the origin we accepted you take it down and build it. The Magníficos tale on steroids. We visualized the structure of organized baseball in its present form. Then we took a few swallows of Chicha de Saril debating in the backyard terraza of Maravilla77. A few minutes ago, Saigón Chiquita's gate sentinel kept sleeping, his face stuck to the concret table, and the Smith & Wesson 38 caliber at disposal to the gangs that patrolled Carrasquilla. That was something else.

Most Baseball clubs have shown the potential to reach the wild card game, at least, as if to keep insinuating the moment is now. It all points to the assumption we're entering the right decade for the leap. What's your utmost baseball wish before 2030? The gift to Baseball or is it Baseball has the resources as it deploys a spectacular show that costs a lot? The gift Baseball may give it Herself, resulting in a mother of a restructure. Organizational and that would be eye-catching. In the middle of the sandwich the ham between the tools at disposal and painting the picture of how the elements mingle in the positive energy of cooperative ownership. Does it really hint we can undertake the task? Can we reach 36 franchises by 2030? It ought to be the gift Baseball can give to herself.

The mother of reengineering and you might have thought of nodding in a no-way fashion, it's precisely breaking it down from the current success looking all the way keeping the balance. Telling the new story in sports, throwing out there the scenarios, and what these scenarios might accomplish. Taking the spectacle to another level.

Who knows if it's wise going through profound organizational changes. Not at this moment of political turmoil and economic uncertainty. It's a no-brainer, thus brings forth a new model at the unseen level of six new franchises and you start questioning if an overhaul will continue to show health in everything Baseball does—not away from how the known success of play-and-profit might adapt to the prospective of reengineering. You agree there are certain things to undertake to capitalize on the correct way to execute the restructure—shall you'd wanted it in a model that continues sharing the resources. Can you imagine having a farm system in which minor league clubs host players from a region, not just from one big club? The predeeding is not an active compartment of the salad toss—it's the example to branching options for the big boys and girls off top might tinker with.

Well, it takes one meeting, and just pointing to activities the Farms magnates can tinker with. To apply and discard based on the situation of their play-and-profit ground. We need to base our conclusions on the fact the fans and everyone are conditioned to look for a pleasant evening at the ballpark with all amenities. Maintaining interest for the game leads the three prongs in baseball's qwest. Follow that bringing the usual income and its distribution binds with the tradition of contributing to the local community, recognized as a permanent fixture in the contribution of the sport to society. Part of the fixture that never will go away is playing on even ground to prevent the bad hops alienate the rythm of competing as fair as just loud heckling from the third base fair pole. No holes allowed in the backyards where the horses patrol flyballs almost over the fence for a four-bagger and a golden glove. The silver slugger out catching flyballs definitely ought to clarify baseball has changed, thus remains the game men think they can play it better than boys.

I'm putting myself returning to the enclaved by San Fernando Hospital, Hospital América and Tandor Furniture off roads with such ackward angles and capacity to dodge traffic. The latest success of managing baseball's aims put the ponder in the 'what if' once your tactical mind takes over, and it doesn't require much other than to realize that baseball's tactical eye got a challenge to think about. Start decomposing your segments—you might take it in reversal—from to the effects of establishing the fielding shift, safe and out decisions by video, the clock and how monetary penalties shape current bonanza. All operators perform at their highest, shall you prepared ahead to dodge traffic. Take a look at increasing interest for the game. In a number of ways suggesting camp establishment and hold of ground depends on the focus backtracking the latest bonanza as reason to undertake major reconfiguration. Multiplying income, as growth is baseball's nature. Here's when we met the product, which it might not want further development, being modest about maintenance on top of all sports entities.

Introduce it as an investment, and it is. Hash the consecuences, and you and I are synchronous that there's no other option. We will expand to Montreal and go west. We'll eliminate what we need to get aside and keep going from leagues realignment and the dynamics you've already preceive. You're just not just meeting the need to separate Americans and Nationals geographically. The need to do away with the present akward East, Central and West divisions. Notice we will fix the season schedule. The total makeup will keep the American League on the east from Montreat to Miami—and the west is vast. The jets won't need to be faster, and you don't have to worry about studying the other league while contending at a 162-game clip for a ring and reign as executrix of grasping wealth opportunities.

About the season, already set in stone and the schedule to fix is the other odd one out. About the other league and about October, the stage when you just acquired insistence that by doubling playoffs berths you accomplish more wealth-type opportunities. Players get a break from the grind, more small market clubs get a chance to the Fall Classic, although the leagues will be packed with winning power and, isn't the actual reality? On an enlarged geographic landscape, on how to manage more play, allowing more teams to compete you also acquire commercial fabric for a longer term. Remember that intensity shoots up then, in postseason. More clubs in a grueling three sets of three-of-five playoffs. Goodbye Wildcard, welcome more dollars for the home team, for the park, and the speculation an intrigue before a likely-intense World Series. Sixteen enter postseason, shall you have expected less.

To that end you might believe this ends the painful thorn on the toe of the average Tom and Jane at the bottom of the operational limits. It's not designed for it, it's unknown, yet it may be known that we've been looking for the decisional template, the aim of this summit. The decision tells operations to take care of business. Operators are also another professional segment of success in case you are misunderstanding that the mention of success just means my vision of the endsmeet of the restructure, unless you doubt the final objective.

Once expansion gets going and you bring the accountants to their intense sheets, it's on the operators. The real orchestrators in winning for the rest of us that thought you don't need to cross-eye with the coach to take take third base if you got wheels. Assume the whole gathering is about winning. Let us depict through the 'what if' epic as the origin to the changes we might need to lock, and it may not be enough. Everybody else focus on the ten-year span. On the advantages and the difficult test of loyalty from the fans. By trying to secure the product, being loyal means willing to lock-in the investment and reap on it like Bobby Bonilla. It's about that sort of intrigue. You win in many respects. Winning considers the origin. Making abrupt changes is suspect of picturing the prognosis of how the restructure of some compartments affects other segments. Revisiting the important segments, this time we won't be taking the whole house of cards down and rebuilding it from scratch. It is not the nature of reengineering. You create a new model and assign resources to it—of course, keep assuming this is about money and money is no problem.

In the US Army, there's something like "you don't have trouble, trouble is the challenge." Well, in the Army there's one direction and it is forward, at least in my seating in my boots. There's nothing more important when landing in unsettling territory than to cave the foxholes.

Looking at the hastily sketched perimeter defense. Where do you dig the holes? You don't want the witch leading the dragons burning the road ahead and the enemy at the gates.

Meanwhile it all must catch the eye of the beholder. To see the potential as point that baseball has entered the positive energy the sports competitors on the sidelines envy. Shall any of the compartments endup single separate reconstructions as result of a magnificent obsession, we won't notice until the premise hints to look at the fundamentals the pillars apply as results of current prosperity. On imagination, maybe, and it may be that someone superior takes notice and calls a meeting introducinf baseball's favorite lineup from her origins and trail:

1. *Bring in a management entity onto the whole of the transformations. Have you thought of Major League Baseball Advance Media?*

2. *Farm CEEOs establish a similar unification-investment pact.*

3. *Convert the selected Farm AAA stadiums where the Majors expansion franchises will be. Think of two clubs every two, three or four years and see how's going and adjust accordingly.*

4. *Bring forth geographical realignment of Leagues, season, postseason for sake of balance—dress the Designated Hitter uniformly to the landscape.*

5. *Relocation of AAA Farm for room to a Majors club offers no option, but to be dynamic like the way of the grind.*

6. *The Home-Grown Academy is the leveler onto future maintenance and advance of baseball's goals, maintaining tradition and embracing change so much as developing young playing tools.*

7. *Can the pillars in the organization provide input? Key internal structures must serve their unwavering support to the game. They always did.*

I was behind the wheel of Scarlet on Avenida Fernández de Córdoba. Turning left at the gas station, the Diablo Rojo buses at the intersection not helping the traffic jam, and the police looking the other way. As I could I parked at the ice cream stand. Began to tinker with the Fabric, to question if the baseball product can be advanced, and put it on paper. The last one, inspired by respect for the sport responsible for a large part of the development of my emotional intelligence. The taste for baseball is the mirror with your image carved to the limit of the depth of the game and its pillars. The vastness of the game materializes daily. The strategy of the game always considers what you can control and pray that the diamond caretaker manages to slow down the opposition, consistent, with simple and effective dirt and lawn tools.

It is not to delineate the difficulty in a game in grass and another in a capitalist universe. It means that as in the game, you give 130% as reward for belonging to the tribal feeling. Adjusting to the design of the contest, you want to get ahead on the scoreboard early, counting on what you have at hand.

Soon, I'd be greeting the Magníficos like in a sergeants major promotion board. The hard way to a different grind in difficult quests, reduced to small details. It was imperative to consider differences, but the similarities to the events in the ball game, very difficult as the municipality loved soccer. What could happen within the next minutes? The time spent reviewing the manuscript. No hurry, better to sit still, analyze and enjoy the trip. That short time gave something to think about how that passion of completing the play with all tools in right-dress-right disposition, can't underestimate the second man in the hitting slot: mentoring, and we guess it's a factor we ought to rank tops, even if you still think "no-way-josé."

It's all built in experience, the mother of the repetitive to refine. Like in the top tool-wailing university: US Army. And in baseball also there is only way and it's forward. Or it be you're still adjusting to the individual pillars of the operation? We think on all courses and actions. To field this one requires a thoroughly oiled glove. Perhaps, the smell in the park gets us the aroma it doesn't have to be hard. Let the play get the ball in it. It's the baseball mind this time.

Perhaps baseball's world has a method of anticipating, as when the ball comes directly in front and the glove is set to automatic, and it wasn't the fielder—had he not been emulating the players that proved the factors of playing and mentoring. There's no other factor players want to accomplish. It is true that there can never be security inside the leather. All that has already been ironed. We are machinery capable of applying incredible power in the upper compartment to the pleasure of visualizing development. That's why I did not worry, in some way weaving the disguise looking for the truth will always remain hard. Obviously, mentalizing victory in this 'special' weaving requires sticking attention to the unexpected, threatening circumstances, identify and sharpen the edges. To pass inspection, you ask yourself, what are we going to sketch and who are the laggers, the good squad leaders and which character projects influence, and this business got a tight hold of employing the elements to envelope mountains of grinding wheels. Luckily to accommodate the demanding pool of players for two franchises every three or four years got a great ally. Subscriptions. The farm is a contract, just a matter of negotiation to open the experiment to open field maneuvers to exploit the good operations in the obscure universe of the farm. Making light to a hidden objective observing that achieving rentability at the expense of employing dynamics to the organizational makeup running like Rommel in a retreat until the tank runs out.

Making sense up to here, so the strange thing began for another cycle to the size of "a protected forum." I felt was seating before that imposing computer and equipment we had at our disposal. Alma dropped onto the project like ring just to the finger. The physical description, indescribable. They did not introduce it to me as I would have liked because of a first impression experience. He wanted to meet Maravilla 77. Making the play easy. It could have been when entering from the brutal vehicular traffic outside by a general public hardware store on the main avenue. I parked the 40 Ford and read the previous seventy pages in my draft in a flash. I needed to be sure this wasn't about soccer. I didn't care—if the athletes I saw playing soccer in Parque Omar played baseball, surely Panamá would have a lot more representation in the Great Circuit, and there was a pack with Tiger hats looking at them.

Upstairs the round table

Ever since I remember, baseball has been a great blessing in my life. Otherwise, I have come to believe that working the count and its riddles means more than a passion. Baseball offers a lot to many. It makes you warm up your arm. It makes you strengthen the tools you know to face the confrontation, which is synonymous with the competitive nature of baseball. It is a matter of numbers, and as they appear there is no other way to deal with them. Advancing or remaining static depends on how you deal with numbers. While at it, let's get used to moving between layers. Don't memories take you back a hundred years?

The emergence of the "Federal League" was a great challenge to the structure of the Major Leagues. That time the supremacy of the Circuit wobbled. The sudden blow of massive expansion put pressure on available talent, and the way team owners manipulated the players. In 1913, there were 16 major league teams. In 1914, there were 24. The activity soared in profits, between battles and multilateral risks. It all started in 1912. The "National Association of Professional Baseball Leagues" did not approve the entry of the "United States League". With eight teams on the East Coast, the USL survived a month, while the "Columbian League" with teams in the Midwest did not open the season. In 1913 the USL lived three days of competition, with discussions about its fleeting eradication. In 1915, the Federal League declares itself Major League, and already came with forty players with Major League, and marketing to 250 players with top-circuit caliber. Because of the explosion in the desire to widen baseball, talent alike, gradually had to improve so that the show went on.

Something curious, since October 1912 David L. Fultz, former outfielder of the Athletics and Highlanders (Yankees) founded the Baseball Player's Fraternity and by 1913 he had a membership of 700. The Fraternity was of great impact on the rights of the players who are already They engineered for the battle with the owners in the reserve system, in struggle for better wages and benefits.

The idea of carrying the battle in shadow of fraternity had arrived. The players dealt with an adviser, and we emphasize that currently the MLB Players Association (or MLBPA) is the negotiator of work for all the players of Major Leagues. Players, managers, coaches and coaches who have or have had a signed contract with a big club are eligible to be members of the Association. It contains three main pillars-a labor union, the Player Choice Group

License Program (the business), and the MLB Players Trust in the role of a charitable foundation.

The Association serves as a representative of collective bargaining and plays an important role in commercial and nonprofit affairs related to the Major Leagues. The players contribute a lot to the development of the sport although during the season they do not have a life of their own, but concentration on playing to win. Otherwise, social works are private ventures. In the case of the players and the teams, the spotlight shines towards the blank in the diamond. Therefore, the achievement of all the components arrived in the envelope permeated by utility, effort, responsibility, love of progress, collaboration, the grace of perseverance and the unexpected of chance. Like the chance that Don Omar Vizquel took fielding bear handed, but Omar made it look easy in his own ways of decisiveness built from a heck of ground-balls and a shortstop attitude.

Preparing this line product of belief that the competitive balance bonanza in playing and on deep corporate foundations may hone the quest home. Because of the combined purchasing power of big clubs in hard, dramatic 162 games-seasons knows how to reap increasingly intense games and autumns. 150 years. A lot of concentrated influence urging for unification counting on what's at hand and the play has to be right. In case the project had been under the object of the relevant controls, we conclude it is achievable in partial or complete mode. Then the idea must include the essence of current success. The model of expanding functions must be parallel to the current model, for whatever it smells as if not wanting to be caught playing up in a cow field. A bad call. That is the handing of the business card with two hands. But the moment transports us to shared interests. There is a lot of fabric to cut. It's like going back to a bad call. It sticks to memory. Never go back to the park or read. The clock of the revolutionary era suggests a new instinct. In the pioneer era, society only knew traditional politics and the economic environment. From the frame of the industrial age, a series of stones blocked the road due to discord between owners and players. Business and art and now it's the digital age and the feeling continues that sport is the latest in the business of forming corporate alliances. Leadership has been perfected in the sense, motivation and actions in an armed goal and tuned with force in corporate alliance. Precisely central is the art of reciprocity in the exchange of wealth. Baseball is financially self-sufficient. It evolved as part of the nature of ball-playing in both sides of the game. In the field negotiation is reigning, uniting resources consolidates power again, in the field of sharing the burden in the constants of goods and services to a fair division of benefits. Would it be the right moment to discuss the arguments in clearer tone. Then, before exploiting the relevant common denominators, consider dive deep into the crucial need for consolidation to respond to the scenario. In case an aggressive expansion begins, we will see how the effect is accentuated for baseball purposes. Surely the solutions to the questions depend on the numbers. Of the comic strips of streets, and the historical traces of the game. Initially, those of unique and varied influence can derive other ideas and routes. Would the Baseball Hall of Fame want a piece of the sandía? Hall of Famers in the neighborhood fit the perfect use of an internal advisor.

Thank God for a park with the amenities above the stands, for the understanding of the team's logo and its courage based on pure leadership and technical ingenuity. Not the least the irremediable factors of the park, to the detriment until the last man is put out. The theme of the park is out of league due its resource-intensive characteristics. Land is expensive, political clout is a must. Stadium builders are used to exploiting the thick bill. The public receives the burden when paying the investment. For sure general management considers another alternative that distributes the cost between the organizational essence a lot more like informal spring training. Very wise to stick the political climate under the vest of the State governor. I hope to go picking up grounders keep a region's sports-proven constituents the key to materialize the profile that management undertook and came home winner. With extreme challenges enter the superior strategies by their level of prediction. Everything hangs between a healthy and equitable negotiation. Somewhere in this sudden evolution in bureaucracy and good sense, the burden must be simplified with changes from within. Of that when expanding six franchises the slice should result in equal parts. For the idea that it is the best complement to a profit distribution system already working perfectly, shall we apply head and algorithms to the cohesion in this contemporary inflow of dollars never imaginable, we would talk about the-no-option objective—is getting back to square one for maneuvers. The beauty of this are the excellent existing methods for distributing the money inflows. Expansion in this way means a chance for investment for those who are already in the knot. There might be certain doubts about the amounts; things that the organization does not stop reducing in cotidiané. Too much lipstick and to the point: the counterweight of a ten-year plan is to formulate a global strategy that strengthens the principles in the Great Paradigm. How do the characteristics of the Plan influence the insiders? Rentability today influxes and floats on all planes and floors with battlefields in crises and solutions in between a game and a business.

The ten-year agenda had an unexpected reengineering perspective. We did not know anything about "soccer", but 16 clubs entering the playoffs would definitely cause enough profits for the franchises, for the players, or simply assign a figure as a cushion for the expansion sheet balance. The sense is to expand playoffs, and it all benefits the collective. More play, more chance of injuries, teams arrive to postseason weary. Yes! You could change the rules; allow a bigger roster, around 28 players, it all balances out after adding more hard, intensive playoffs play. Maybe a decent change is look at the playoffs deep considering series of five games the standard and don't tinker with the World Series. Obviously, the team with the higher wins in regular season should obtain home advantage. Do money, time, weather and players' endurance match the worth of a longer season? The answer can exit from the inside. More playoffs, more dough to distribute, and there's no other two activities where players feel more comfortable—playing ball and passing their experience to the talent behind them. Players, in collective contribute greatly to society and most of it not noticed to the mainstream. Large salaries as the blindfold, and perhaps, if money is no problem, then the will ought to be high challenge—and it will be.

There is a wing flying high and with power, distance and frequency very responsible for the current bonanza. MLB Community takes care of everything that permeates the altruistic vision. MLB Community contains her credit. Her deployment to social support in formidable panorama. Assuming around her activities and achievements not only depend of grinding the initiative manipulating space, time and being decisive about it now, but preparation for the unexpected is the logic. Point to capitalize on the positive of the commercialization of the channels in marketing with no interruptions nor the accustomed threats and how they are surpassed. No excuses, the move must be as forceful as a long season. Then, expansion improves competitiveness and brings wealth while cementing baseball in the community-for the fans and those with a broad perspective. Lastly verify the positive rebound.

Therefore, the marketing and management in baseball are events enjoying expert domain, as professionalism outspreads among the allies and down to the fan. In all areas, the analysts at the head of the monitors, and the rest of us studying the effects as the East, Central and West divisions dissapear. The Wildcard has its charms. And if we replace it with a series of five games, there would be a chance to bring the wool to more cities and regions, and it makes sense. Intense postseason money, fans paying for tickets and goods with prices sky-high. More important, greens that could afford a piece of expansion, since you invest now, and in ten years you earn the big return. Like Bobby Bonilla's retirent story, to be told if matching precedence is the interest. Otherwise, we can explore the neighborhood to gather how difficult it is to win the World Series, but that has been the traditional reality. No past expansion team experienced the advantage of partnership forged by collective support from various angles. Optimizing the predominance of players from the newcomers of the minors back to the neighborhood will indirectly increase the unified value in the locality. The support we can build by developing the local cloning of baseball with the HomeGrown Academy and the connection of all youth programs could be the jewel that gives tax exemptions without resorting to tax manipulation. Keeping the house clean.

The players' job market and the rules to compete allow the teams their broadcasting rights for negotiation and sale. Infinity of intangibles such as the imminent international draft and innumerable negotiations on the talent that is the core to win games, then series, to bring the league pennant home, and play and intense postseason and World Series. Notice the intensity during playoffs?

There are even metrics to invest and spend a specific amount of money for each victory. All this, stuck with resin to the domain of players waiting for modification and empowerment. Negotiation and conflict management, thank God, they are a strong one. The gift of the system is a check from the Central Fund to do with it whatever it is by order of the distribution agreement. Anything can happen with a good dose of luck, and do not miss the chemistry of the stars entertaining in the stadium and via digital devices. May the wisdom of those who create bliss for all be the professional way.

The book you hold in your hand gives a glimpse of how the era of knowledge gives way to the era of concept, honing on the same loosely organized set of facts, observations, experiences and insights that set baseball apart from the rest of sports. Amid the charms it's all about thinking, that is a neurologically and therapeutic way to live a magnificent obsession. Mine's the mixture of humility and daring aided by some research, enough not to bore you, but hopefully the most relevant expositors of the game ought to nod alright due their previous notes and publishings. Take George Castle, for example. In Baseball's Game Changers, he notes that in 1900, upon Ban Johnson and Charles Comiskey rebranding the Western League into the American League, it took just the right timing and nerve to attach fans to dollars. It'll never change, so it's natural we evolve along counting our resources. Isn't that what Branch Rickey said? I don't know. Hole you didn't lost it. It's on purpose to get you back on track brainstorming the emplacement of the HomeGrown Baseball Academy.

HomeGrown Baseball Academy

"The players's dreams of glory are no more compelling than the scouts's dreams of discovery, of seeing the crystal through the carbon, the future shining through the present."

~Kevin Kerrane
Dollar Sign on the Muscle

Thinking on it, it's like the mother of remodelations. Baseball gathers 30 powers embedded in distinct sets of rules as the field keeper applies chalk on straight, fair lines. Watering the way to greener hope. A window to the endless expanse past the foul poles. However, mumbling about where to diagram the diamond is unleashing the blueprint in full force. Or at least a quick simulation of baseball's further potential. In the process of getting the ducks in order clings to the challenge of watering the ducks. Or is it dependent on the ongoing robust prosperity? To put boots on the ground in a lapse of ten years—expansion of six additional clubs is the ultimate. The stepping-stone to widen the game's principles, keep baseball leading the rest, and ensuring growth. You just start believing on a few bouncing marvels: prosperity, alliances, and professionalism into the new dynamic of collective ownership careful not to impend the current dedication to complete shut the inning and brin runs home. Then things begin to complicate, and because the achieved competitive balance suggests putting the resources in play, to simplify any confusion for sake of the point. It'll take materials to build it.

In a 10-year timeline, expansion, leagues geographical realignment, modification of the regular season and playoffs, creation of the HomeGrown Academy, and bringing forth an Expansion Management Pilot. A neat set of three capitals that has me sort of confused and the impulsive idea the EMP is the very first step to implement. She will do the thinking, the organization, the brainstorming like if dissecting this book from rear to the branches any additional neural conexions may get you going nodding yes.

Not fust for sake of it, imagine the EMP is in place, intending to land the perfect flow to design the whoke chili and watch the assets take off into the journey. The EMP ought to become the middleman safeguarding the collective investment. The executive manager of the new franchises with a fully developed plan to make them competitive, and by the way, the idea of getting eight clubs to playoffs matches well with newly faced clubs, hungry for the ring.

This is the perfect stance to have the thinktanks that the EMP can hire to exploit al the fabric. Getting to realize the fabric is accomplishments and potential, as they are poles from the same obsession. Figure then that play that guides itself from the lessons-learned in the old 30-club ways, achieving a respectable level of prosperity in that ten 10 year span I've been trying to slide across your page gazing may not mean nothing.

Well, didn't want to leave off that baseball's future blueprint also calls for creating a new model inside the old. Sounds wacky? In the first three years of the decade, you could field the Montreal Expos and the Las Vegas Stonehands. Give yourself three years and plant the San Antonio Broncos and the Utah Highlanders. Thatr's right, upthere in Salt Lake City. Hopefully we will complete the journey with the Oklahoma Bisons and the Portland Merchants.

And you are wondering why the desert. It's a hole in the west. Ok, no one handles more wealth, more young talent, more new ways to sense winning capacity than baseball, and now, the Expansion Management Pilot. Mainstream-30 does and to your instant inquiry whether we will be tinkering with the dormant theme of monopoly, we will be waking it and luckily Baseball has been exempted from monopoly since 1922. Insinuations the wake of the monopoly debate might be a showstopper, no chance, the business is established downloading profits. No chance we fold a perfect source of income. It just makes us think pulling from the thought everyone is making well and we will not stop pointing to the marshaling area in the next expansion.

Ok, you want to be illustrated on how your season can go unscathed, no obstacles than those your daily grind boldly overcomes, and how about the statutory and reglamentary drives? It's all part of the contemporary battle sketch. The rest is to crank high gear as usual into the carefully planned haul for maximum return. Basic and simple—play and profit—apply the winning principles, and no other definition of professionalism bats leadoff in this lineup. Baseball has great allies, and no one has figured out a mainstream alliance will execute a multiple expansion faster, swiftly, prepared to solve forthcoming dilemmas and challenges, and put nine men in the field.

Unless the game gives credit to all the elements and invite them onto the offensive, through the Expansion Management Pilot. The associations responsible for growth don't move beyond television deals, concessions, licensing and sponsorships. Take for example, as Major League Advanced Media made a deal with each separate club and returned to each part of the investment not used—made a collective agreement and is part of the structure. It's fair you'll be advised to do the journey unified, and you knew that from the enlightenment in every day during days for great ballgames. How much is your collective reach right now? You have the right to know the blueprint calls for cutting the pie in equal pieces— according to the reach of influence, it has a limit. Of course, the investment takes precedent. Working in unified scope everyone may be assigned a piece of the puzzle. How much is the combined reach of the owners of stadiums in Majors and Minors? Shall you invite them to join the caraban, it's wise to weight baseball's principles: create interest for the game—profit—competitive balance—and contribute to the society. It's a four-way intersection with all paths leading to the notion the product must advance. The principles might be the source might to breakdown the assignments if you think you're off the hook.

Why is the Home-Grown Academy so relevant? Her value stands on the reality that we don't need an expansion to implement the long-missing piece to get the youth in spikes. In a nutshell, the HomeGrown is baseball's influence for the young, and this time the professionals lead with unmatched game mastering approach. Linking the parks, making that youth leagues in the market region identify themselves with a unique effort from the Majors club. It's not a thing of lack of money. It's awareness there's a free school near the park and club you admire for their hospitality and winning aura, while the professionals disengage from how the Dodgers are doing, from a hell of a season end-strech for the Cardinals, from the Astros difficulty to be beaten, or by the Twins became the Cinderella and who knows if they wear the ring. Glued to such feelings the HomeGrown brings professional polished utilities to the municipality. I hope soon the concept become the strong edge of the phalanx—shall tjhere surface the need to extract one single dynamic from the mother of restructures. The HomeGrown is most valid to explore due there's plenty of subject-matter expertise willing to ride the wagon. Become the spearhead of baseball at conquering new frontiers getting everyone's attention that the game has arrived in the municipality to assemble all youth in and around the ballpark. Why I keep thinking professionalism has no boundaries? We'll soon see the Pros reach their second dream—to pass on to the generation's important society-shaping experience. Why such a sudden leap to maximum use of leadership? Because they are professionals and professionals come from the community. They dedicate themselves to mastering the game in organizations with experts at the helm—the singular difference, they can project the outcome of the play based the singularity of professionalism. It's just the quickest way to remind the world that the professional seed has more power in his hands than the universe perceives. Players sense their incredible showmanship of completing the play, and playing flawless is the supreme influence. They do want and need recognition for gathering the kids where the grass is greener, because their fathers, mothers and uncles showed them the way to the bat, the glove and the spikes. Much else in store, it has to do with the journey.

Don't overlook the awesome success in Dominicana, Puerto Rico, Venezuela, Curazao and every other place holding the baseball academy fever. Professionals run these unique schools and all thirty major franchises regard the concept as indispensable. The HomeGrown will match proven success. I don't mean teaching the game in a full department-of-education curriculum like in Boca Chica or in Carlos Beltrán Baseball Academy. It can be done, but the objective of linking the region's youth leagues will want to close that loop. The HomeGrown, althought imagining awesome baseball clinics and all preparation to play in the deep Circuit in a few years, concentrates more on linking a common relationship among excellent programs like Little League, Babe Ruth, Urban Youth Academy, Revival of Baseball in Inner Cities and everything that puts baseball as a generally healthy activity to feel and smell the scents of the game that kept you late at night visualizing tommorrow's game.

While I was developing this part I came to visualize the impact, and because this is sacred ground for the professionals, it's them who'll decide the approach. I came to respect such influence on the point that all they would want clarified ought to be whether they want a pilot program in a region, but if so, remember we are working an agenda of one decade. Most clubs would want to implement the HomeGrown since yesterday. The earlier you atract the talent into the local club sphere, her development be easier to follow, of course, with a team of scouts. Remember the HomeGrown will knocking on your touch as you devore pages questioning if anyone ever launched the idea. She's a tool built by each Majors club in charge of creating more unity among the youth leagues within the market region. And yes, it stands worthy a search for the least, a difficult level to share skill, utility, programmed discipline, sense of humanity and returning the sacrifices for being able to reach stardom. Nowhere is that easy. It won't be pop corn, either.

We must accept and exploit the capitalist features of the game we love, and never leave home the social endsmeet of the game, while the air of change gets purer. Assume six expansion franchises by 2030, but what are the events you may face before getting there? You just let yourself go and experiment its entirety or a fraction, and who knows if the HomeGrown ought to be the spearhead of the phalanx, while the cavalry stomps on any charging elements, hopefully on the flanks as not to disrupt ongoing deadly assault for kingdom reign. There's always a reason for advancing the product. Only the field gardener could make you pay attention. At the advent of exploding populations and clubs perfecting their operational and financial process and fortitudes, on this day and age, managing change falls in place in numbers calculated by common sense and fantastic machinery. For Baseball, the lineup is carved with the tools of skills, knowledge and money. Expansion and realignment are on the horizon. Never has been the moment to look through the window of prosperity to cement the top ranking over the rest of the professional sports. The air of change gets purer; it's just on how one paint the lineup. Baseball is way ahead in independence of clubs. Players now adapt admirably to the fundamentals, to clever winning showing off unique individual tools in teamwork. Professionalism and baseball fervor on and off the field is on high. Merely by observation, that right there proves this other journey is possible in unified fashion.

However, I didn't discover dog rubbing healing until a few years as I was really clunkering the Olivetti plotting ahead, then viewing the future shaping the mother of baseball rearrangement. Each major new objective ought to depict a number of answers to a number of inquiries about even where to begin. If you're wondering if instead of arousing intrigue inducing impatience, we refinish the persuasive facts. Pick a first question at random. The question is to whom ask it, thank God for simulation and field exercises. The familiarity of thinking in time means having natural ability for choices. An attempt to know and predict what's next in case the hook for a decisional template left your layer. We hope any strategic move may be fingered based on analytics that measure a happier future.

Is it the latest market-encroachment penalty? Who affords more stadiums? What is the public's sacrifice? How about the reaction of federal, state and local government? Do the markets possess the investment threshold? Naturally, the typical decision template may ask for intellectual dissection of the project. Someone inside may hint opening the revenues book. Out of the blue creating the Expansion Management Entity is essential. Balance may be questioned as if a 30-split ownership do need a control valve. That imperative, as a major departure from the traditional, relieves the worry that some clubs might obtain unwarranted advantage. In itself, the topic is a sequel for who thinks management entities operate superior in sports.

Things heat up in the western frontier. Baseball may look isolate—it might not be surprising the odds place the diatribe onto positive vibes. Prosperity the son of capitalism is from now in charge. It appears the secret of negotiations at the fortitude of the structure has been the power of sharing, not just intuing to checkout game-theory and yet is never too late to take off. That's just the panoramic setting into the leading incognitos.

What's the route to eliminate critics and attract them into the voyage? Now, here is a good one. The existence of the Designated Hitter causes some disproportions to the game. It would have to be in both Leagues and extinct. Game theory at its bests suggests it. On the surface, it's all about salaries, team expenses and maintaining the caliber of competitive play—most likely earned clashing with change, the random part of the game. This is not the mission to be solved in a single viboac. It can't be solved in just a few sittings, and if it might accord stronger labor settlements the blessing. It shouldn't leave us under the major conundrums of remodeling stadiums and establishing expansion farm clubs and their grinding to do what the Farm does.

Paquito Montañez   *28*

But first, lead off and get on base. Here comes higher creative branding in titillating form that may put the Expos, Broncos, Bisons, Highlanders, Merchants and Stonehands in big league competitive nature. The road to expansion and alignment begins synthesizing the discrete or disparate elements of success, as achievement represents the single most important fact of potential. Figure sometime more than one powerful baseball executive opens this book. Instantly he or she discovers that 'possibility' means synthesis of bang for the buck, since executives got a nag for such things. The matter by then, there's no turning back, but to keep the pulse on the unique of total asset visibility. Clubs see the resources clearly as management is individual 30 ways or so, at the tune of unique business philosophies. Envisage the actual robustness on the play and profit spectrum. The health of earnings suggests augmenting the power of wealth and keep ruling field performance like sports never seen. As balanced one can adjust an additional notch, in a bottom-up view, the powerful elements in Economics known as trends may be leading factors of success, and potential. It all can be worked out in unity. The items too large put aside and see how the pillars assimilate changes with no turning back. If the first impression of the project is not reasonable, it must be adjustable and adaptable to the fundamental principles of future prosperity and how one can assign focus to the completion of the blueprint. Working from a showcase in simulation and modeling, a chunk of opportunity in expansion and realignment may be the solution for strengthening unity, growth and the larger role baseball plays in society.

It's all up in memory of information. The road to expansion and realignment ought to begin on a timeline. A band that requires planned answers to strategic questions. Perhaps the Commissioner, advised by the internal elements may lead an expanded vision of the project. In terms of illusion versus reality, most of the homework is in the bag. Most of the research has evidenced results. In Best Interests of Baseball, Professor Zimbalist touched on significant patterns of governance, which its coexisting exposed to our separate but cohesive functions. Whether one holds premises of negotiation—like an agent's duties and influence—be the Commissioner using authority vested in his office to induce cooperation. Out of the batter's box in a hurry, huddling together in unified direction is to gather the ultimate partnership from the disparate. Zimbalist noted "there is a massive potential synergy in controlling both a baseball team and television." Reason to affirm the idea hasn't moved other executives from the static for 29 years. Precisely through synergy, the fabric of new dynamics is 180 degrees in an era when influence exerts in strange ways. That said, governing a club, a league or in this case, shaping towards a visionary landscape managing and molding a decision from thirty different perspectives and thirty different personalities take more than a little skill and patience. One meeting can crank it all.

MLB has an opportunity to become a better investor that creates value for those interested. It can do it contemplating its stakeholders' domains, in the way she does. As the expansion franchises become contenders, a platform of indirect support (enhanced sharing) can produce costs reductions. In economy scales, the reasoning that the equity piece flowing towards all MLB mainstream clubs will be benefited, so the shared effort ought to be its motor in the win-win arena. Let's pretend the Commissioner had asked for the Fabric Strategic Scorecard. Naturally, the thing had been brainstormed since receiving the 'operations order' in unique perspective suggesting a critique meeting. Otherwise, out in left field observing, searching for two or three courses of action with having to propose one, checking every angle that will hurt you is a must. The unexpected.

The idea is to kick a reasonable analysis, as the crossroads of goods and wisdom distribution means progressive proximity to the usual partner that continues tagging along. What simpleminded formulas the elite squad would explore is up to the forward-looking elements to begin unfolding the usual win-win scenarios. But how is winning so crucial in grabbing things in the background and incorporating them to further the play and profit context? Even the role of taxes flicker in the backdrop adding the notion there's got to be another tactic to make the use of available dollars stick to the effort and benefits. Baseball has a collective bargaining agreement which at a given time was designed for balance. At another, money shed into the pot moves out seeking to prevent bankruptcy and maintain competitive edge.

Twenty years from the last expansion, small market clubs have outgrown imbalance. The sharing-agreement at its worst has taken cash off the rich franchises for sake of a healthy Central Fund. At its best your highness proves high-paid rosters are no better than low-earners. Baseball has surpassed a 29-year threshold of growth with all goals certainly achieved. Now is the right time to plot on the board of growth using the tendencies that got you upthere in the first place. Is easy to underestimate the targets and terrain to traverse as wealth moves between hands, and before you realize arbitration season has arrived. The draft is upon you. Beyond municipality and the network of businesses and social work, baseball does it well. Wouldn't be curious to hand pick a couple of those spheres and disarm them to see what they are made of. In the hyperbolic vein in the like of Thomas Kuhn's view, baseball historical changes depend on breakthrough and transformation, progressive and cumulative in dynamic forms. Speaking in these terms, the development trends around baseball's events seek the goods spread beyond territory. Anyone liking the sport or part of it knows being in favor of greater good means seizing the political entry for as long as playing competitive and doing senseful practices precedes the worry to go on the offensive. Adherence to the social virtue in the golden rule is to concentrate on current level of power, never underestimating who's going to afford formidable opposition while in unison fighting for the same goal.

The money is available, but just about everyone has an economic opinion derived from individual perspective of harnessing the meaning of hardball markets, the environment known as survive or perish. Imagine how doubling the clubs reaching playoffs creates the subtle conviction that baseball has not exploited prosperity at its maximum capacity. If the project, under the object of the relevant controls, concludes the track is achievable range, then the potential of the economic power is formidable fiber. We should see wages two decades ago. What it costs to go to the park or appreciate the game with television devices. We must remain curious enough to discover something new among the prestige in the game. There is no need to look beyond 20 years to predict the expansion can be executed in 10 years. Just look back at the last 29 years. Drawing from the organizational memories while MLB rose to the leading position in more games, in prestige, better paid salaries, more greening programs in service and commitment of the sport and the young. Playing talent is developed at an early age, and the list is long. Don't be distracted the fine print of understanding what is coming depends on formidable cooperation. Brutal re-engineering?

The game is still transforming. It is organizing loose ends for the better. Policies and new processes are essence of depth concentrating balance in the doctrines of importance. Balance with better talent and science in the eyes of commerce and playing to win. There's a lot of balance, opportunities in entertainment and in the sewing and selling of wool. You ask a current operator, and you hear the perfect narrative is stored and cooked in the data banks. Well, since MLB has a compartment to store, its people are doing remarkable work. This allows you to put yourself on the side of the experience and assess yourself inside, where things are clear. In other instances, while time travels, outsourcing and transforming depends on three commons: technology, team thinking, and current performance. The rest measures and applies the shortcuts for play that hunts the best of the series.

The concept of ownership, while MLB is the sole owner of expansion, may refer to the creation of favoritism. Not if MLBAM or anyone takes the contract as the Expansion Management Agency, it will be entrusted to fill everyone's piggy bank. From the lair with all armor in gear, the idea does not deny authenticity, for the trends indicate the time has come. In the same way, appealing to leadership and trying to grasp an idea about prosperity requires more than a test to understand the knowledge and capacity that permeates in bad times and in great moments. Since then, has reigned a desire for results that live the banner. However, there are great obstacles to the emplacement of a separate-like sector of competitiveness, and many lean against the obvious restrictions, if there are any, and bureaucracy the showstopper. Jaron Lanier, in his book, Who Owns the Future, wrote that fundamental questions can be declared in various ways. Only a handful of answers will emerge, a few are possible. According to Michael Spence, winner of the 2001 Nobel Prize in Economic Sciences and writer of The Next Convergence, certain types of economic freedom have access to markets and finance, and its governing system allows people to invest and belong to companies without processes requiring excessively expensive approval or having direct restrictions. Kill the bureaucrat and don't worry about what you can't control.

Who in Baseball would put the finger on the first step to enhance the product, ready or not enhancing the signature of the game at all levels and depths?

2 |
Hit the field running

"[Pai] has special shoes that make marks on the ground when he walks. His arms and shoulders seem to be able to pull a palm tree off its roots. His face is hard as the blocks holding the wood boards of our house."

~ Bengie Molina with Joan Ryan
Molina: The Story of The Father Who Raised an Unlikely Baseball Dynasty

Lore says Baseball as sport has its origins in the Taíno *batu* game played in Cuba and throughout the Caribbean. Spanish chroniclers who traveled to the islands during the conquest and colonization periods provide evidence of this activity. The batu game was played at the batey, a ballfield, court and ceremonial ground. Players used a ball made of resin and shaped leaves. As recorded in Cuba, in some cases, this ball was hit with an instrument similar to an oar or spade. According to Cuban linguists there is a relation in the origin of the words *bate* (bat) and *batear* (hit) with the corresponding words *batey* and *batu* used by the *Taínos*. Since bateys were located on the geographic borders of *cacicazgos* (tribe chiefdoms), ball games probably served to deflect hostilities over territorial disputes. As if in the act of survival, winning the contest granted integrity to the tribe's territory, and let us assume it was all about winning and keeping afloat the Kanoa and surviving the flesh-eating Karibes. Lore says so that the game is about winning. Everything is done in order to win the game, because winning the game is the ultimate goal. The reason you play in the first place. The purpose of the game of baseball itself, removed from the outside world, is to win. In the path of a greater future, winning must be kept in perspective with the other valuable aspects of the squad you bring and knowledge of the opposition. It's a summer habit and one may enjoy showing off our dexterities to advance our merit, our product. Why not go into expansion? It's the most prolific way and a chance to adjust to greater dynamics. Don't you see it? Baseball at the beginning of a great transformation. Wait a minute, it has been through change for a while.

No doubt baseball is science and art putting forth broad foundations with varied abilities raised to superior level in habits. Imagine your strength is associative, baseball is like that, like in the fun of brainstorming and after grabbing the cup start thinking on the bullpen. Imagine the way is in comparison to assuming it won't be a leap in one attempt. It'll be too bureaucratic. Of course, simplifying it with the use of technology is the way. You want to move this transformation very orderly. If we were to change, couldn't we plan a meeting? That is why we have convened, although it may be about the tools at your disposal. You may perceive it as with the forces consolidated on high ground for better thinking of the move. All ducks in order. Ready to leap if the money rings.

And it made sense in an already distant epoch in 1994. The year Professor Andrew Zimbalist wrote Baseball needs the 10-year timeline and expansion to overcome the players and umpire strikes, and that interests and power struggles were buried in the grind of that era. Expansion would be the manual of play to balance the last American frontier—our dollar at work. The sharing-agreement wasn't in effect, and a competing professional league installed itself in Florida. Baseball wasn't talking to himself, among its superb and flawless performance from the trembling structures responsible for results. Then, as Major League Advanve Media, the umpires and who knows if more secret permanent associations came about, let it go as evolution to this thing of now. It's the collaborative key, the giant part of sharing the wealth. That's large. Being an internal feature, will it be too hard for MLBAM to contract the management of the six franchises? It makes us think. The ten billion in value giant may represent the file to sharpen the rough edges of the idea.

The Big Leagues had survived serious falls; players and umpires strikes, fans booing. Baseball people—it sounds influential, capitalist, and grinder of that science and art in batting, fielding, running, catching, throwing and scoring the most runs—all factors of a chance to win while trying to simplify the deep into a simple game. Compare Big league people 1994 to 2019. Who worked the difficult projects to overcome that sort of negative energy?

I will not do it, and we can introduce that associative strength of yours parallel to the resources at your disposal. Chance for success, that we will hone equally tracking the competitive nature of big-league grinders that continue shaping the game. The competitive nature involves technical skills in the depth of a game of chance. While at it, a thick business hangs over the game. The instincts and motivation to succeed in a contest, a series or a season bring individual performance in association and the solution has been harnessed a long while. Play and consider the game as positive energy. Trying to win is to allude to the goal imposed by common effort. For being full, wide, deep and a beautifully varied and intrinsic game, it is evident the desire to uphold to superior performance suggests the curiosity of a creative display. The Sport, amidst its falls and bounces and teamwork at such magnificent resonance of pride in a simple game, must use the strength acquired to move its product over the geographical horizon expanding dynamically and decisively in unified form.

How about we assume that expansion is the most accurate direction? The last years in this decade eyewitnessed the prodigious for baseball. The experts predicted great accuracy towards the difficulty of entering the postseason. Hold it there. Suppose baseball wants a new face or modernity takes its course forcing an expansion. The Bigs are comfortable with the current structure, but change is always a hidden boundary that may bring us to a column of opportunities and much curiosity about everything else.

Powerful organizations must grow, although risk permeates their surroundings. Look at the descent and rise of oil. The world is somehow chaotic, but powerful conglomerates thrive. Every day new associations are formed in which someone is in charge and many in the chain delegate actions to Sabermetrics and financial geeks to connect the key elements to execute in spite of restrictions and making hard decisions based on availability of resources and internal laws on the eye of the beholder—soundly delivering in high octane—give credit to the operators. The resources allocated are the powerful use of assets according to their capabilities. It means the imperative to take precise and correct action exploits the value achieved. Are you ready to leap?

Acting has been the traditional chronicle recorded in the annals of the big leagues. The creativity of the game always turns out to be the stranger off the polemic. Already the remainder of the puzzles are in the confluents's chamber, the balance is to keep the interest for the game high, and credible and profitable. That and the manipulation of the political legitimacy of the markets as the profits double and improve by the minute and on the hour. Notarized agreements manifest assembly from regulations giving fruit are really, really imposing. Let the strengthening of work actions remain the credence for healthy relationships inside and with the fans, while the government is the multiplier on guard. Nowadays more people understand the benefits of sports entertainment in an environment rooted in political and business finessé. Alliances and actions and use of time sustain the rollercoaster of the markets.

Imagine a spring morning after expansion has been completed, to celebrate the dynamics until then. In attendance, all the owners flanked by the operators in appearance of aggressive gabardine raising the stakes to another level. Lots of discussion about what the fans and associates have to say and how far the availability of talent allows—if indeed—reaching forty franchises might be plausible. Nothing ought to reverse it—money talks. Chances are that someone reminds the crowd that baseball is ready to distribute mind, body and soul for this to happen. The assumptions are mixed in the debates questioning the nature of the strategy for the leap—systematically facing the common risks. Common because the cat has been domesticated. The issue must inform that you can move forward with these ideas, with the ideas of the people in the media, and the expressions of the Commissioner of Baseball have hinted we're near taking the show around the loop of new suburbs. The general managers utter the cotidiane to motivate team preparation to reach an intensive October. The front offices just waiting for the orders of deployment. It's not so difficult to find out why during past expansions the owners acted individually establishing their own franchises and dealing with the failures in their own boundaries. The tortuous road of executive meetings in alliance to exploit all business opportunities. In the same vein, wouldn't it be off the wall awarding the League Pennant to the winningest team during regular season? The beginning of an epic in regular season feats.

Casting back geography, the structure of 30 clubs rooted in fierce competition looks like random design in selection of logos and feelings. The opposite side of the coin is tradition. Clubs are bearers of reputation and amidst former clashes between owners and players—right now it all is peachy prosperous. However, the growing sentiment about maintaining rivalries and rentability in high governs the way against any attempt to modify the structure. That is good, control is a must. Rivalries are beneficial, new rivalries benefit. Change is inevitable, and general questions are another order to understand and assign the scenario in numbers and figures. Then the solutions will be lessons-learned as in any historical context permeated by success in the play-and-profit spectrum.

All we know is that baseball is a competitive-cooperative affair sustained in winning as its core philosophy. You win at home, on the road, in the hearts of the fans, in selling extra tickets, in the bank, in getting the taxpayers to finance the stadium, in getting arbitrage and free agency to get us more money in contracts. The owners want victory in the field and in the freshness of a corporate format motivated by money. Winning is even the essence every time the talk is about media, communications, entertainment, loyalty and branding or developing the franchise adored by the fans. Beyond imagination, it does not take additional awareness to see that expansion is the sure way for baseball to be more prolific. And there is no exact way for the narrative. In fresh perspective, although it may look extraordinary, searching deep answers to deep questions before introducing more on contracting the inside element to safeguard competitive balance requires a hard decision from baseball's power brokers. Let us walk along the path of ideas on reform and how a broad descriptive. Hopefully, the future will draw us the road map and the trip will be made reality, and witness the trail of opportunities, and investigate, even if each concept does not reconcile the disputes that may and always rise and until the fat lady sings, there be more fabric to figure and divert onto your own idea using your gut instinct. There's good balance between great performance in prosperity applying the prudent formula of taking the bull by the horns. By expanding the geographic realm, changes to the norms will surface. Think it all remains a thing of running structure that guarantees balance as the ultimate objective. You keep it and what is the problem? There're just challenges. For better balance of the objectives, assume is to exert weight on the core. Finding an optimal decision on it may and will branch ways to improve the competitive-cooperative signature.

Among what has been said, such a competitive structure may exert great upheavals in the affairs of the markets of the franchises. Do you have another opinion? Part of the additional challenges. It might be necessary to see from the fan's scope when throwing overboard the illusion of playing fair in the East-Central-West divisions system. That concept does not satisfy the whole picture of fair play without turning an elbow of the leaders in the decisional helm. Everyone club in the League must play everybody the same number of home and away games. Expect that Leagues realignment is due and shown as to complete analysis of the laundry list of aproval and opposition you'll contend with.

About league repositioning we gain that season itineraries need to focus on balance. Remain playing 162 games because the advent of a longer postseason requires depth stamina. There's much to add to relieve the effects of the Injured List and the way the rules of September offer more latitude to use every able and capable player in the extended roster you just perceived, and it's alright, it's the nature of an expanded signature. Increase the roster during playoffs if you think the perception matches the same little baseball lineup of priorities in the decisional diagram to deal with the unexpected.

With sixteen top-finishers entering the postseason will not prevent baseball from reigning among the undecided. Earlier hold of control is the power of wealth exerting pressure to remain static. Preserve the status quo for sake that resistance and the usual detractor insists. No adventures or bad loves that truncate prosperity shall be part in the fabric. In absolute negative posture, to intervene as if living in a perfect democracy thinking the political nightmares inside the Circuit might be just the biggest showstopper—in spite of the influence over the competition.

No Tweeter war can't insinuate it'd be no ballgame tonight. As the result of no contest under the lights, not being able to play it's a degrader to power, influence and expertise. Figure then the opposite—don't strike, enhance play and you may be confronting your own analysis. As of right now, no other sports entity continues to fly high, holding strong through the most difficult times and bouncing back better than ever. However, how could we avoid losing focus onto new spinning ideas—ideas must attach to the vision of reorganization cautiously and cognizant of adverse outcomes. What is that that may trigger reflective dilemmas? Such train wrecks.

Show me the money in patience. First step to spearhead the mother of reengineering. First step to change the likes of managing small ball and the era of WAR and the modern philosophy to delegate part of the decision to the proven in taking the game to the locality, one now global capitalizing from the sort of constant that prosperity endures and leaning by the fence in right field don't prevent one fromn looking at the messenger. Bringing expectatives to the local fence huggers. Are the Big Leagues at the gates to the march into the mother of challenge? Impossible it'll happen. We'd had to definitely lay out the scenario playing the odds.

3

A walk in the park, and it is not

"The plate in baseball represents the point of intersection where the lines extend at an angle of ninety degrees, theoretically in perpetuity."

~ *William M. Simmons*
The Cooperstown Symposium on Baseball and American Culture 2001

It wasn't debated, the first pitch was thrown to open a game that didn't even start until the call of play ball. It's a process embedded in the playing-schedule. That precedes the chalklines. Predicting better visibility of the contribution of clubs and players to the community, may be that of talking about the opposition, but the utmost effort remains sharpening your tools considering that in professional parks playing under 100 percent diminishes the fun. A simulation, and if you don't share the fun and the smell of fresh-cut grass, the smell of cowhide and the smell of powdery resin won't kill you. Return to believe this must conclude a subtle message, if your memory clouds, it is because the product of play and profit intuits that virtue of winning merging the colossal and the bulky to understand the game, we think we comprehend as humble and simple. A unified effort with contributions from many sides, some with corners to be polished, never perfect.

We hoped not to underestimate the crossroads of making radical changes by chance, consensus, learning and business design. Really, does it apply to baseball among its sovereignty? Doubt does not prevent you from simulating at least the agenda and its style. It can trigger the unified decision (the one we do not expect due brutal it seems). We would say that the total makeup of MLB will not suffer changes that negatively affect the activity of winning. But transforming the structure and obviously, some processes relevant to the increase of competitiveness, which is good. You want the visitor hunger for shaming you before your own fans. A lost at home. It would be interesting taking the measure with fans in mind. Exploiting the income potential and continuing to do the best Baseball does. No scratches, superior to all other sports entities.

Ethical to formalities the shackles off. We are ready to investigate proven facts to be used as answers to assumptions in their maximum efficiency. For prior reliability, Baseball will make its independent sense as to the size of the new goal. Making sense of oneself in expansion can transform the distorted from the straight. Relegating to accurate information to look through the ideas of advancing baseball as it dresses and how the intrigue might deliver a creative initiative. It forces us to formulate our own sense and decide, because time doesn't pardon, and it hurts. It comes very fast like pan handle over your head. To present compelling impact, we had to match the ideas with the facts before marriage of calculated words. Returning to the origin knowing that convincing the influential pays attention to the evolutionary path of success as a science, art and cooperative play. A broad but replicable challenge. Manageable? Why taking it so deep standing beyond positivism picturing the horizon. Because it's a matter a distinct approach be pulled from the bag of experience. When is the game more intensive? Assume is during the planning stage; as the precise moment, like when crossing the foul lines into the diamond looking for position. Roberto Clemente told a chronicler from Pittsburgh he was the greatest player ever taking to the difficult agenda of doing it all inside the field, in the basepaths, and in and around the batting region. I reckon he was referring it gets intensive thinking at 130% of productivity. Crossing the line his part of the play became focus above and beyond. As he crossed the line, he understood his tools to complete the play. Appreciating tools is what is all about. Then afford to speak one's mind at the precise moment to assess cat-like instincts to go get balls in the deepest and farthest regions of the outfield. Momen honed his sure on the bag throw, it all had been planning it over leaping over the fair lines.

And the timing couldn't be more precise; time does not take prisoners. Step off the batting box and set rubber and cleats inside the three-foot line to first base with no hidden advantages. For a second, what makes the Bigs the main candidate to carry out the modification of its structure? It is a definite and profound challenge, and it gives us something to think about. Back to 1994 I bet Rickey Henderson hated not sliding at 3rd base. He had to go on strike, and it had to do with that darn Reserve Clause—about labor qualms. And keep imagining we are ready to deploy today's metrics and all that numerical detail believed responsible for the harnessing of the art of playing as a science. It must also consider the human wonder of putting the meat of the wood on cowhide if the deliveries allow. Let us compare that had we deployed the playing-development earlier and massively, and I don't know how much we need to emphasize Baseball is game and business. Big challenge, teamwork above the bleachers. The Professionals know it. While when Rickey Henderson was the master of swipe, Professor Zimbalist of Smith University proposed with verified data that Baseball's solution ought to be expanding to forty franchises in ten years and he must be thinking the the advantageous contemporary resources and conditions favor his old idea in folds. Thus, it can be hard. In 1917, a Bridgeport, Connecticut munitions laboratory recorded Walter Johnson's fastball at 134 feet per second, which is equal to 91 miles per hour (146 km/h)—a velocity which may have been unmatched in his day, with the possible exception of Smoky Joe Wood. Today's metrics are way more advanced and improving. Figure Walter had sore arm, because Ty Cobb said that Walter Johnson's fastball cutting through the air made and extremely uneasy sound. Hopefully if these scientists convened the art into the science of picking up bullet speed won't make you feel in the zone of discomfort—in your mind there's nothing to be restructured. You can also be a rebel from belief, and it's alright.

4

Money does matter, and the trends are dynamic

"At the end of the day, responsible management means more money for everyone. And almost always, more shoes".

~ *Rick Horrow & Karla Swatek*
Beyond the Scoreboard: An Insider's Guide to the Business of Sport

The day, in some memory compartment. The morning, when waking up late. We were imagining with common sense and evidence. From there it depends on to raise the level of the ballgame through expansion. It is worth incurring risks, the interference to the daily struggle of the game in double faces can be affected. Slow filming and negotiating skills, resulting in forcing better deals. Anticipating expansion will happen, influential streams will favor in the domain of interests. Reality presents us, among history, the current barbaric economic production in the golden age governs itself as the narrative of secret wars for control. The interest in control led the day of resentments, invaluable mistakes as lessons to perfection well known by professionals. Secret wars for Control, not upping always maintain your humor alive.

However, profit turned disaster into prosperity, and everything turned into win-win moments. The era has arrived where you reveal those lessons and apply them to the collaborative method. Believe it or not, the actions of distributing the fair booty to the productive effort surpasses any other current of the push of the competition.

Creativity in bringing the game to the armchair and super wide screen? How many shoes did we sell? Do we care about remodeling stadiums, we would say, uniform around 42,000 seats? The figure comes from thinking of the minimum to continue in position to go back to the postseason. It's believed, the Athletics and the Rays got the least sitting chairs. There are two stories, same outcome. The franchise stays, begins getting anew, and the wheeling and dealing gets hairy. Look at the Marlins, Derek Jeter at the helm of decision-making. As if we didn't sense mentioning the crucial path of leadership that is built inside. Is what you prove in the long term. When was the last time we stopped by the checkboard to review George Brett's career statistics? Baseball is that way, as if the so much broad aspect of a sport. We can take the answers to what makes people of baseball another key to the final test. And if the idea returns the debate that broadens, would it bring a salary cap? You do not notice, because of the incredible control in the nature of the business. It is also something already the Players Association has under iron and with the plan up its sleeve. Salary caps cannot be subject to evaluation. The spectrum of the business and the existing balance in the scale of organizational power do not allow them. The income distribution system is considered a salary cap, but the least harmful. It is soft and manageable.

And what about the current prosperity? Think of another way to see the glow. Very important we don't straggle away from the facts until answering questions with questions, no major decision will take us forward looking for a tool of security. What's safe at about the lineup Mike Sciossia may impone? One thing is sealed. We don't count Albert Pujols out. As weird as it may sound, since Ichiro made his historic entry with the Mariners, there has been two places to look for glory, the all-time, by season, trophies, and the advantage to have Albert Pujols in the lineup. The performance boxes of Alberto and Ichiro Su-suki, as their best, prescribe attention to the game. The inner works of the pillars holding initiative in the grind. To instill that hunger baseball made us steel, something else comes to mind. The game must go on. Meanwhile best advisory is bred within.

The ways to earn money are versatile. No one wants to talk about interrupting a warm and substantial remu-neration for playing ball in capitalist territory. It is a cur-rent, capitalism, what are you going to reorient. In which there is little control. You think about leadership and the powers of studies, the unique human knowledge and the broad perspective of the experts inside. The factual in the reference, in service to the honor of not tracing the re-mote, before maneuvering tactics in the unpublished segments checks the current condition. We already said that this is the cause of using the fundamentals in the field and on the stands and selling and ensuring that the ab-sentee fans of the stadium see the pod by digital devices. Win-win situations have shone the trends. But where does the money go for paying so many hot dogs and brew in the range of $8? We are sure a lot today has changed. If there was no barbarous prosperity, it was not for the sup-port of the fanatics and the business chain weaving every second while you read and you are passionate about un-derstanding the fold.

This is history, now prosperity rules. Today the influ-ence is focused on cooperation. Those battles for domi-nance almost throw the game by the cliff. To the contemporary premium, the machinery to make money enriches everyone. According to the references inter-calan the advance of gains flowing to all, we begin to im-agine those who take the wool. The attitudes and fortitudes of sharing wealth have turned to the positive. Obvious and safe, it is not worth concentrating on the initiative. The risk is worth using the same control that almost derails the train of wealth. No initiative separates from the contest. 162 games are still the norm. Arriving and winning the World Series is another type of war of powers putting pressure to follow without many changes in the structure. You arrive if you do not suffer scratches, if the "disabled list" does not slow you down. Keeping the current contest according to the rules and the summer manual, hope in autumn teach the smell of more tickets for team effort. The intense during the postseason. A world of competition, luxury, risks and opportunities. That, without leaving precious anecdotes on the outside, the risk is another dimension for another dissertation with equally deep angles, in each restructuration. In the MLB reorganization, too high. To figure future generations absorbing the debt. At the highest level, it must be like eating a peanut, because at that plane, analytics is of caliber to show the route to easy play completion. Baseball is on high octane in the constitution of human analytics and that inspired by tradition and the connection of the foundations in game and business. Beyond imagination, you do not need additional awareness to realize, growing additional clubs is the safe and feasible way to enlarge baseball. Suppose that everyone wants decent contenders, rising incomes, willing to get out of the fairy tale building new stadiums. Consider the cost to the fans, who pay to support the game we love, and no longer listen "we are moving the franchise to another side". It matters better an investment for all, in the end everyone would be owners of expansion. Money does matter.

5 |
Leagues realignment

"For almost a hundred years, the universe of baseball has focused just on the border of Pennsylvania and Ohio".

~ *Fran Zimniuch*
Baseball's New Frontier: A History of Expansion, 1961-1998

I t might be extreme to emplace two franchises every two or three years, but brainstorming on it ought to be the first leap:

Montreal Expos & Las Vegas Stonehands
San Antonio Broncos & Utah Highlanders
Oklahoma Bisons & Portland Merchants

It's radical alright. At the beginning of the 1990s the theme was about money and the unity of the owners. In 1993 the average salary rose to $1 million, from $ 371,000 in 1985. Timeline of a victory for the players, and radical changes of impact to bring the party in peace while the dought kept arriving and distributed to the ever-increasing receptors of profits because the investment had been wise. From there, the distribution system, the Collective Bargaining Agreements surged to ensure competitive balance in the stadium and in the bank, and still different worlds in common orbits one another.

Jon Pessah, in The Game, says negotiating in unexplored waters requires resolving to the rhythm of the tide. Bud Selig owned the Milwaukee Brewers. I was hoping to be the "Baseball Commissioner". When he arrived, the magnates were at war, the players with the Players Association didn't allow their elbows twisted. Within the ranks of the owners, factions, the game faced challenge from many origins, many interests.

At the time, George Steinbrenner, the Yankee CEEO strongly opposed the distribution of income. George opposed luxury fines established to prevent abuse of the rules. The Yankees were the Yankees. Mr. Don Fehr, acting as patron in the guild, and the powerful Association fighting against the salary cap the magnates intended to impose. It all turned for the better elevating Baseball to the top and the success handling that kind of situations into prosperity tips the balance towards potential of multiple expansion through a unified effort.

In matters of organization, MLB has no problems but management of complications in challenges. We do not believe that we lack resources if we accelerate their concentrated power. We live in the era of resources. Speed and agility modify the physical and mental environment to develop game around the diamond. It would not be uncommon for contemporary society not to benefit from creative methods as indispensable for learning to move forward if you find yourself in good standing. Naturally, in the felling of the "yam" of ball and bat, speculation is the trend, when going down the same hill a while ago.

Then, following the capacity and the canyon of between the middle and the difference, our rear sights are focused on the exit of the canyon. Create conditions, with the tremendous condition of professionalism, extended to the ends on the bleachers and glass offices with the smell of beers and "french fries".

The design of the higher order scheme does not have

to lose continuity of the current contest, and the last ingredient of achievement permeates the entity. Apply solid perspective from the armchair to create playoffs with intensity, without underestimating that the latest on the avenue consists of a very intense postseason. Behind this intensity the Machiavellian experts applied the power to the situation. The seventh game of the World Series. In the game, during the 2017 season, Lance McCullers Jr., the tallest and "short" muscle mass from the mound looking at the powerful Dodger lineup, no less, in the refuge of the Dodgers, the Chavez Vineyard. We never knew if out of control, by the impetus to dominate with pitching in, Lance Junior got two balls to Yasiel Puig and two to Justin Turner. The dangerous rookie of the year, Cody Bellinger, McCullers gave him three strikeouts. Clear. It is healthy to add that Puig and Turner came with great displeasure to have tools of power to the wood, and surely the intensity of the moment playing at home would be opportunity to get the game to the visitor from Houston with another great garrison. You take out the big three of the lineups and the rest bring the "screwball" with swivel without marks to the swing box. At the front of the bat and low as to plaster dead in the box.

Intensity or Machiavellian tactics in the direction from the cave of honor. From the beginning of the game there were people with economic influence for maneuvers outside the league. Today the influence floats on all planes and floors with crisis and solutions.

Preparation and execution for a game, the series, the season and the not so easy coming up to the postseason requires putting faith and hope in the obvious attribute, but not delegated to its maximum extent. To the leadership, the reserve cavalry, it has not really been given the value in its main desire. Leaders work hard preparing new generations to maintain their competitive recreational home.

The task of preparation and execution at the level of 162 games and the business that it entails today is very advanced with expeditious analytics of massive data and human capacity is responsible for talent. The basics of Murphy's game and handling and the theory of giving the best you can in the field, with the character adjusted by a sport with humanity and its merits, just in case. It continues undertaking and guiding the activities under principles, and seminal regulatory ideas on the medal to the caste and superior level in baseball competition. By radical a proposal does not detract from the merits to conclude is a matter of crushing the offensive with the estates and put the accounts clear. Would some consumer books be opened in the franchises? We do not know. But to the other spectrum, it shows another aspect for insight:

AMERICAN LEAGUE	NATIONAL LEAGUE
Toronto Blue Jays	Detroit Tigers
Montreal Expos *	Milwaukee Brewers
Boston Red Sox	Chicago Cubs
New York Yankees	Chicago White Sox
New York Mets	Minnesota Twins
Philadelphia Phillies	Houston Astros
Baltimore Orioles	Texas Rangers
Washington Nationals	Colorado Rockies
Pittsburgh Pirates	Utah Highlanders *
Cleveland Indians	Portland Merchants *
Miami Marlins	Arizona Diamondbacks
Tampa Bay Rays	Las Vegas Stonehands *
Atlanta Braves	Seattle Mariners
Cincinnati Reds	San Francisco Giants
St. Louis Cardinals	Oakland Athletics
Kansas City Royals	Los Angeles Angels
Oklahoma Bisons *	Los Angeles Dodgers
San Antonio Broncos *	San Diego Padres

*Expansion franchises

Notice the beautiful geographic layout. Many rivalries are conserved. The schedule can be balanced. You can jump to a post season tournament of sixteen. Interleague play is no longer required; unless we think of interleague playoffs and that'll be further chances to discuss it.

Expansion has pillars to be treated between the philosophy of unification. Out, you have to see the institutional registration card to achieve such great success. The success planed by a spectacular level of prosperity. What else do we locate for the growth initiative? Seeing the components, each one has contributed its granite in this great beach of unique sand, agile and calculating now without much criticism. Sizable prosperity clouds any doubt about the reach of organized baseball. The idea is to establish six expansion franchises in eight or ten years in a property model where MLB exercises the right over all new contenders. Why Las Vegas Stonehands and Montreal Expos? In two to three years later we might think of the San Antonio Broncos and the Utah Highlanders. That will close the loop with the Oklahoma Bisons and the Portland Merchants; all in ten years. These clubs will be sole property of all MLB; except you'll need an administrator. And what if we put the growth in a mannequin where MLB gives a collaborating organization the keys to develop the future of the six new franchises? It is correct that whoever wins the contract will do everything possible to develop these fresh clubs and promote them to seek postseason action and keep Expansion clubs afloat on the ups and downs of the markets and the bureaucratic notion of an organization already with charismatic, not divisible tools in hand. Such would be the instance all the actual clubs will be equal owners of the investment of expansion, and because other depths like stadiums, farms and teams of operators suggest brainstorming for a while, we can not deviate from engaging in conversation followed by a meeting.

We must invite people in the Bigs domain, and naturally, we suddenly imagine the internal analysis of the entity. Analysis of her components, as they make the best deployable tools. Inside, the elements domesticating the environment, and the markets in good position. Will the elements be worthy of participation in the decision to deploy baseball to another level? We still have to resort to the last collective decision in a very diversified world (thinking about the composition of who owns what). Property has been and continues to be the priority. Suddenly, we see the collective power of the Bigs in hard contests and with some uncertainty because of the width of the idea. Juust realize from here on meat on the ball means handling the sound before it strikes the catcher's mitt. Perhaps we put a bit of dedication dedicating ourselves to the big 30, knowing the torrential in the farm system is separate and quite dimensional business to capture human skills at stake and in business. We do not see any indication that the expansion clubs compete unnecessarily even with the unfit to reach the postseason. If there is, let's discuss it.

We do not object to the roles of the Commissioner and the Executive Board are extremely important. We perceive the collective authority among clubs dictates to attack the last opportunity based on the disciplines that lead fabulous prosperity. The current leaders are the engine modifying their thinking based on reality as they see it, and they continue to own their own prognosis based on experience. Sometimes, because we are aware of the intensity of the game and the table of positions, we do not realize that the owners of the estate and stadiums have their corporate reach. They do not go fishing, but thinking and exercising action on the opportunities to sell tickets, arrangements with luxury boxes, attracting the fans with a team rich in depth of bank and body of relievers, and amassing business forces. This is the endeavor that tries to answer deep questions to so many safe compromises to emerge.

By the way, the pillars have more strength than the average tom, Dick and Harry care about very little. Fortunately, the media puts everything on the air so that we appreciate capitalism to its maximum splendor. The "good-looking" image of today's athletes has an impressive impact on society. Something distinctive today is that the patience to see the result of good foundations and practices, is the result of questioning who was more successful by practice: whether Brooks Robinson, Paul Blair or Carl Ripken. Difficult to quantify but verifying the individual performance report for the team. Since we live in fantasy fueled by sports, sports must empower the same fantasy and advance according to their abilities. It would only subtract a meeting to talk about tickets. In the end, everyone receives the portion according to the amount of the investment. Decide the acceptable distribution of resources to put in hands the work.

Who dominates the business spectrum in partnership and institutional part? Trying to say who I believe will take the command of expansion, captivating intrigue, would not indicate Major League Advance Media (MLBAM or BAM) has gone down and up the path, and already that patrol is line 1 in the scheme tomorrow. The scenario projects BAM as the Operations Entity if the rest of what is coming to land in the decisional theater of the convinced.

MLB has no problems specifying contracts or agreements. You could assign control to an Expansion Operations Entity. Assuming among the functions delegated to the Operations Entity, it would be the authority to develop hard clubs in the field and broaden profitability for all those who invest in expansion. As a semi-autonomous authority, the financial, economic, and operational point and subordinated to the Baseball Commissioner and the Executive Board. Without advancing to raise suspicion to the enemy, expansion can bring headaches, and all reengineering is worthy of ingesting the magic pill, breathing deeply and analyzing the initiative. Yes, it is a matter of reengineering and there is no other, as you attack territory when you are at your best. How did Bobby Bonilla turn retirement salary into exponential? On 1 July 2001, the New York Mets paid him $1.19 million. And they will do it every July 1 until 2035, as part of a deferred contract that the Mets negotiated with Bonilla after the 1999 season. Instead of paying him $5.9 million that year, the Mets owe him nearly $30 million in the course of the deferred contract. An excellent plan to match expansion, considering many retired superstars enjoy the same pension terms. The story and that move from Bobby is the living example and reason for investigation. In how the collective financial and economic dominance would agree—there is no other way—but deferring revenue in the style of Bobby. Of course, all the new gear takes its parallel flow to institute the game to another level in geography with the ability to withstand the commitment of blank that gets more intense every day and attracts more interest. Here the intrigue is about who, when and where the actual scheme of expansion begins. The powerful and influential networks with technology bringing the game to the sofa have the right to compete for a cut; and even it seems to be the name of the icon. The best advice resides inside. The Major Leagues should be the example to other institutions for experience in crisis management and economic scope. There is leadership, the expectations inside mold the potential, and on the outside, to go to the park to break the diet, to witness the game at another level. It is not like peeling a mango. Forced changes depend on risk mitigation. Experiencing both constant risk and reengineering, the perimeter has been mined in prevention and conditioning towards the unexpected. If for any reason it results in bad strategy or bad disposition, the other spectrum makes you indisposed before the den that you considered safe perimeter.

No pack of wolves devore you like in Hollywood

I still remember that rainy afternoon in Parque Omar. Ruperto narrated that going down Loma Coba on the Pan-American Highway, he thought of the advice from his wife Idalia before boarding the Chiva bus towards Nueva California, Cerro Punta and Volcan of the Estado Independiente de Chiriquí. He had spent fourteen years pretending reviews of forest life. Writing reports on how the politicians and corrupt corporate were slinging the budget from the pocket of the citizens. It had been "fertile ground" and he hoped not being expatriated from his country. Was he betraying his country? The American establishment recruited him in country information domains, in that instance, all aimed at benefiting the wishes of the American government in the foreign affairs sector, adventures in national security. Luckily, I heard for legal defense, one lawyer graduates every eight hours. Transporting beaks and spurs from the highlands joining Provincia de Bocas del Toro, and acting coordinator of bloodshot tournaments, lately had been squeezing Ruperto's dopamines and the whole set in the olive-drab compartment above his neck. Maybe he should decline membership in the horticultural federation and executed plan B with the report on fortune tellers and healers in the magic of the yam projects. Like the current government administration, but the reality considers the solution up front if there is no way back. While the perspective became promising, spotting the concrete city at the height of the Thatcher Ferry Bridge, at some point would have to wander in Parque Omar, the golf course which during the military dictatorship was seized from the affluent oligarchy. Surely there I could listen to Ray Sepulveda singing Fool of the Hill while the baseball obsession was acquiring depth.

We went pondering the time for expansion has arrived. The clock told us to eat a Chinese rice from Don Lee on the first floor of Hospital América. Since the broadsheet is wide, the author from the highlands first had to settle another heraldic bearing. It was just after the general elections of 2014. Ruperto wanted me to explain the synopsis in understandable language. I followed the track and bought two ices. How could I not offer the Don for his wise decision in pursuit of a country study. We sat on one of the wooden benches. Almost behind, at seven o'clock, a rather chubby man speaking in Italian with the other man, taller, well refined like if ongoing embassy chores. Suddenly, Shorty got a call, he resembled a mini-version of Tommy Lasorda—highly likeable. He continued to speak in Italian and to my expertise the conversation turned to the business of owning a piece of pie overseas. Perhaps the matter was circulating around the lost wiretap machine; the Israelite-built one. According to Didier, the undercover that now Jibaro Hampshire, the U.S. Marshal protected under WITSEC. Franco Nero could be from any agency or country, he brought us the first instinct that was Cuban with good training in Hialeah. Ruperto almost finished his raspberry icee and indicated me with his lip to get online behind the Mister with the Franco Nero-like individual, for sake of repetitive image. I greeted him and asked in English if he was Italian, and he returned in perfect Spanish he wasn't. From the corner of my eye, I looked at Ruperto, and it only occurred to me to say that lately the chatter in the city is in Italian. He smiled and I told him that Ruperto is about to publish Círculo Cero, his latest novel. Before witnessing the man's most mocking smile was that Tommy ended the call and they followed the ñaqui ñaqui in the language of Calígula. Before leaving, they both learned that Ruperto's novel would be about power struggles, money laundering and the government's wrapping. The triple government ascendancy had already ironed the laws in favor of politicians' influence and in full control of the national budget. Hence the gleaming of teeth and the burlesque smile from the Cuban. Leaving the two men on the way, Ruperto advised them: be careful not to end up characters in the mother of the Italian novella; the one dealing with the radars that don't pickup speed boats and the Fenestrón choppers. Serious and fearsome space the park of the Fool of the Hill, I said to myself. My head was on something else, and that part of Círculo Cero would be exploited in the future like a digital map with a key in hand, only after verifying if it's true: that Didier could have been one of the Magníficos and I knew who due to his expertise stealing bitcoin. Then we took the walk again and we started to develop ideas about expansion, not before the Magníficos had the essence in the glove. For the intrinsic details, a meeting was on.

The Magníficos mean unification—the baby and the genes of teamwork, and soon they would return in front of the curtain affirming that complete collaboration completes the play. I guess the Fool of the Hill might be the fear of the challenge; it's something to rouse the feathers. Figure the Bigs want to clarify the local, national and international visibility. The Office of the Commissioner and the Executive Committee have broken the code of not only taking advantage of the accumulated knowledge in the universe of data—from the singular ways of mining said data—assessing the state of the income; checking the competitive balance; and seeing the real effects of taking advantage of specific predispositions that maintain a focus on potential. In particular, serving as a link to so many wealthy, each with personality, involves meetings at the tune of Sigma 6. These are great assertions, but unquestionably with courage to think at the disciplinary level these people maneuver. Deducing whether MLB has the ability to install the Montreal Expos and Las Vegas Stonehands as spearhead of expansion, it leads to conclude the competent, dominant culture of the rudiments (like the Central Fund) is a good start for the sum of the parts without detracting from considering the reach of the thirty franchises, the farm system, or that keeping stadiums in full swing is duty of professionals used to the grind and grit of it. It all consumes huge resources, but collectively ought to be a whole lot less painful than the current individual ownership. Undoubtedly the concentration of great alliances reigns over professional sports entertainment. The discipline approach to perceive we have been moving to change. To the habit of the dynamics, the food of modern times. Feeding as decomposing the huge collective lever to organize without the season suffering imbalance. Without forcing the need to stop the rise in salaries and maintenance costs, real at all levels. Inflation is looming. The decision is not as easy as peeling a coconut. The power of baseball to deploy the place of tomorrow rests on the last decision, and it has to be unified. The scenario seeks the application of the invisible hand that favors the interests in productive activities that promote prosperity to vast segments of society. In the usual habit. We would say that no additional thinking intued by mentors can't resolve before consulting with the Commissioner and the Executive Board. They are experts in their specialties adjusting to institutional design. A matter of receiving feedback for another tournament with spikes and spurs, where fragrances smell of commitment. Playing superior someone will follow this debate by experimenting with the Designated Hitter in the National League. If you pour that cream there's chance for a lot of cheese, that said a reference in the backend, in the little squared cockroach room. To be specific, the DH is fertile ground with a larger figure to spread opportunity to the young, to the proven and the lover of hauling more runs home. First, we formulate a conceptual model that allows us to study the context of the challenge, identify specific objectives to define all the variables and logical relations. A flow chart that guides us, as external and internal observers, to partial reductions by matching the properties of the fabric of baseball. Super! MLB has proven to be intelligent and shrewd in a game of ease that does not come from nowhere. If it were not for the analysis as history transforms, it's from the profound vision; from origin to trajectory, to success, that facing the onslaught of the business remains intrepid. Baseball has made it look illustrious.

Beside this 'new scouting report', elsewhere Murphy says oil had a decline, it is said to have been jumping and now says it's superior. It must be the unexpected from the markets. Nor are we going to overlook the recent tax reform law that favors the corporate universe. In higher spheres, jumping to the move asks to reorganize the structure, the business and the relations with the allies. That the daily picture is not affected. Since the rest have history and chronicle, there are even metrics to invest and spend a specific amount of money for each victory. All this, stuck with resin to the influence of players waiting for modification and empowerment. Given this, we can not avoid problems and challenges. Negotiation and conflict management, thank God, they are a strong one. Now the small clubs receive a check from the Central Fund to do whatever it takes, courtesy of the clubs with prolific markets and the income distribution system. Anything can happen with a good dose of luck, and do not miss the chemistry of the stars entertaining in the stadium and digital devices. May the wisdom of those who create wealth for the players not be lacking. They also need to be empowered and everyone to win. Now that prosperity goes well, who dares to put aside a portion of the luxury fines as seed for expansion? Prior to the details and an explanation to the Monarch, it would be convincing and logical that the project be based on global leadership, on sustainable growth, and a deep perspective unifying the MLB properties. The establishment of six franchises today is more complicated, as increasingly powerful organizations play leadership roles in the global status of baseball. Decision-making always depended on influence and interests and nowadays it is harder to navigate the bulk of the corporate crust, especially when profits in other industries depend on the success of the ball. Luckily, the entire MLB structure has voice and vote, which at another level could all influence radical changes impulsive to improve interest in the sport and increase money in the Central Fund. So, assuming another major objective is to distribute profits according to the investment contribution, which must be equitable to avoid turning the balance towards certain teams with better or worse market.

Definitive historical and future rivalries should always be part of the game. There shouldn't be bad blood in the middle. Examining old and new rivalries, technically, puts you in the observer's slot. We have begun to evaluate dollars from the mission. It always does, baseball does more before 0900, than most competitors in overtime. Very difficult to leave out the DH. Big Papi Ortiz piled a lot of firewood as Designated Hitter. Equally, you never discard use of the seventh sense in the reason the executive should delegate the matter to those responsible on the side of the game. How about an electorate, a majority among all the directors, coaches, coaches and even the clubhouse mascot; a vote to see if the National League adopts the Designated Hitter, and additional chance to give more credit to Edgar Martinez as a dangerous hitter. Edgar covered the area of blows to the Louisville Slugger quite frequently. The free agents of the future may have a part-time job, but it is not worth discarding reality. In the cave of the Majors, it is true, picturing a bat in the lijke of Manny Ramirez ought to be a great commodity, and it makes you think the DH is here to stay and expand.

Pondering to understand what is not defensible does not prevent us from checking the suspicion of doing everything is a road map. Putting our scribbles on the boards in the sand of the paradox. Here scoring, in opinion, no campaign leader proposing to move the machinery a few plains and hills accepts being offered the maximum in resources. Even with good advice where operations are hard as a coconut shell. This to think smart, not hard. Half dead laughing, we immediately learned we wanted to present-even if there were four stripes pondering where the sun is hiding. Perhaps a simple allusion in that sports world ticket, gives the guidelines on the move. Power and influence do not drift, and it will be interesting to swell the reason. In some future idea, the road map would not be better than shaking the growing magnet of the postseason, in interest for the game, competitive balance and benefits to the collective. If expansion felt like candy, the sour be those oppressions to a system clearly healthy in cash flow. Thing that people there interpreted as dressing room talk while checking the non-negotiable numbers need to take the proposal seriously. In the realism that we chose—precisely the objective of taking advantage of the workshop for a while with a chance to learn something new. Options come and go and are part of the process when deciding anchored on power and influence. Then, the hunt to impose influence resonates with the political process and social state. Perceive the pillars of baseball can, in a curious way, exploit the unified strategy to put the product to another level. It'is not a coup. "The professional leagues are cooperative ventures outside the field of play, with teams committed to a number of gathering practices for collective identity." Words by virtue of Scott Rosner and Kenn Shropshire. The Business of Sports book. These gentlemen verify that in sporting adventures the contenders have no way out, but to cooperate to see the ticket blossom.

The Professionals continue to define the pure existence of the rules, doctrine, and fundamentals. Now the chips on the table are the television, radio, commercial endorsers (tennis-shoe guy), those with licenses and sponsors, recent ones with hard work and understanding of the cooperation in the unique narrative by the essence of which in baseball there is balance in another pinstripes suit. The secret of winning is already known and emulated. Would some consumer books be opened in the franchises? We do not know. But to the other spectrum, they threw us another table and we already saw it. It immediately causes a lot of enthusiasm. In advance, Andrew Mearns' Internet writing gives reason to think, as he makes constructive criticism of another intriguing experiment. In 2015, Jesse Spector in Sporting News magazine wrote driven by fresh rivalry in Texas and the Astros playing in the American League. One could suggest realignment where the Yankees and Mets, and the Cardinals and Royals played in the same division. In Baseball America, most recently, in October 2017, Tracy Ringolsby expressed that expansion could trigger realignment. "Rob Manfred, the Commissioner, speaking in Seattle brought hope to the people of Portland, Oregon-that Portland is a place with potential for a larger franchise." In fact, since 2003, the state of Oregon approved a partial sum of $ 150 million to finance a stadium in case the Expos moved west. The concession is still open. According to Ringolsby and Manfred's statement, "there seems to be consensus that the ball is heading towards the configuration of 32 teams. Such a configuration would cause realignment and adjustment of the game calendar, which would offer MLB to address the concerns of the Association regarding the demands of playing outside the home and on free days ".

Since we have been building a box to think off of it, the complex order of any future expansion must emerge with simplicity in timely realignment of the leagues. It would be necessary to see from the sight of the opponents when throwing overboard the illusion of playing evenly through the East, Central and West divisions. That is noticeable to leagues. That concept does not satisfy the grand scheme of competing without traps or in quicksand. In the league realignment table, you can see from the first impression that you need a balance in the itineraries. Let the regular series remain in 162 games. If 16 clubs enter the postseason it does not prevent baseball from remaining indecisive. It is the power of wealth exerting pressure to remain static. Preserve the "status quo." No adventures or bad loves that truncate prosperity. In absolute negative posture, to intervene as if living in perfect democracy. Giving the negativism chance to formulate the antagonistic to know what it is and the arming strategy.

For now, no other sports entity continues to fly so high, holding strong through the most difficult times and bouncing back better than ever. However, how could we avoid careful thought of spinning ideas that could trigger reflective dilemmas? Antagony invited. Pondering to understand what is not defensible does not prevent us from checking the suspicion of doing everything is a road map. Putting our scribbles on the boards in the sand of the paradox. Here scoring, in opinion, no campaign leader proposing to move the machinery a few plains and hills would accept not having the maximum resources. Even with good advice, where the operations are not co-conut shell either. This way of thinking hard not to work as a mule.

Disrupting the game?

Establishing oppressions to a clearly functional system that can unbalance the cash flow is not the intention. Thing that there interpenetrated in the dressing room checking the non-negotiable numbers need to take the proposal seriously, and what arises there, there must be solved. In the realism that we chose-precisely the objective of taking advantage of a workshop for a while with a chance to learn something new, it does not prevent us from exclaiming if you are going to improve with the favorable conditions.

It would be through the synthesis of the changes that we were soon to expand thinking that both the season, from the game itinerary, the designated hitter, the postseason and the option to implement the broad role of the HomeGrown academy under the tutelage of the Expansion franchise as a full option. Options come and go and are part of the decision process. The time is always right for a meeting.

Then, the hunt to impose influence resonates linking the political process and social state. Perceive the pillars of baseball can, in a curious way, exploit a unified strategy to put the product on another level. It's not a slamdunk. "Organized leagues are cooperative ventures off the pitch, with teams committed to a number of gathering practices for the collective identity." Words by virtue of Scott Rosner and Kenn Shropshire. From the book The Business of Sports. These gentlemen verify that in sporting adventures the contenders have no way out, but to cooperate to see the ticket blossom. Major League actors continue to define success by the pure existence of rules, and the doctrine of principles in all relevant disciplines. Now the chips on the table are the television, radio, commercial endorsers (tennis-shoe guy), those with licenses and sponsors, the recent ones with hard work and understanding of the cooperation in the unique narrative by the essence of which in baseball there is balance in other lime stripes.

Let's do this as if it were the mother of sports reengineering. A sensational scenario No matter the level of wealth, its distribution, the distribution of the players, the works of the support staff to the franchises. That parrot does not get in the middle of the road. That is, by setting aside value, we seek pleasure by developing action that undermines elementary procedures by disarming the present moment, separating what is known apart from what is clear like water, and what we can boast so that the interlocutors can decide in the near future.

Assume if the product should advance through expansion, we would need to skip the tradition of expanding only two clubs and wait decades before looking to the horizon with another plan and usually by then, the stadium and the spreadsheet are exponentially expensive. The teams value all their talent as trading cards and consequences during picks in each draft, but this is already part of the business. The ball seems redundant as for expansion of two franchises every two or three years, being aggressive now to harvest long before 2030. The redundant thing continues unless we begin to see it in the potential of the structure. The trajectory has been rocky but the important thing to deal with in the complexity of competing came to be business diversification and diversity in the field. Now the game has turned multilateral. That's why the finesse of falling into a diamond knowing the opponent does not stop being priority. Behind the curtain the insiders have seen the local environment to know where baseball is a show and where it is projected to raise the bar of success. Seeing from the armchair of the disciplines, none is bad unless they are applied with the same gift of contemporary success. Grinding it requires you to be a sharp one in finance and in other skills to reinforce the importance, before the challenge. Imbuing the emulation seeing the moment in the General Manager's scope is only an invitation to the water hose behind third base.

In gestures of curiosity, may the opinions propose a Study Panel thinking about the resources and how to distribute their reach. In the past the Blue-Ribbon Panel made its merit. A report of 187 pages, the genesis, in the year 2000, concentrated in a new system of income distribution improving the balance. According to E. Woodrow Eckard, in the Journal of Sports Economics, "there was a marked recent decline in the balance of competition. The alleged cause is the increasing disparities in team income and payrolls driven ultimately by the size of the market. Consequently, radical changes in the economic structure of the game are necessary, mainly composed of new restrictions in the labor market. The report, however, does not present evidence of a decrease in the balance of competition or of a significant link between market size and profit. The present study sought to provide the missing analysis. Although the competitive balance could have decreased in the American League, it improved in the National League. The difference is important, since both leagues are subject to the same structure of government, that is, the decrease in the American

League was probably due to idiosyncratic causes. In addition, there is (at most) a weak relationship between winning and market size that has not worsened in recent years."

Intensity or Machiavellian tactics from the dugout cave of honor? In fact, from beginning to end we were suggested to know the endless work of the experts inside. From the beginning of the game there were people with game, economic and operational skills with out-of-league maneuvers ready to discharge. Today's influence floats on all planes and floors with crisis and solutions. Baseball exploits its greatness through preparation and execution for a game, for short series, for the grinding of the season and the hope to the-not-so-easy postseason. Once you're qualified, turning the odds much easier. How you maintain the force that took the team to claim a right to compete and hope randomness comes your way to win it all. Shall it due to delegating to capacity and to its fullest extent? If it's the norm, there is a start as you usually know the leadership, you're one step ahead from accomplishing the tasks you assign, and there's no other option to best advance of the baseball product.

6 |
Time is upon us

"If baseball teaches us anything, it is to have faith that history remains to be written, and that there is always hope for what the next season may bring."

~Daniel A. Gilbert
Expanding the strike zone: Baseball in the age of free agency

I wondered if instead of fomenting impatience, we had made the persuasive an easy arrival to second base with no slide. That was something else. Who do you want to sell this idea to? It was what came out of Ruperto's mouth. To many people, it was my first inspiration and first naivete. We only need to visualize the structure of organized baseball. Then we took a few swigs of Jamaican saril debating win-win scenarios in the back of the Maravilla77.

That day, in some compartment of memory. The morning, when waking up late. Around the same kiosk of canoes walked the Fool of the Hill. The first time I saw him caressing a model of finely crafted fighter aircraft packing stuffing. I offered him something for the model, shrugged, and realized the pod was not for sale. Worse, the skinny boy with Negroid traces did not have the ability to converse. The juice dispenser that he studied at a prestigious aviation academy in the United States told me. It was brilliant and overnight he lost his mind. No notion, he manages to survive in the park. On two recent occasions, I saw him pushing a block of ice and groceries in a supermarket cart at the Casa de la Carne in San Francisco. At least, the people of the pirogues, before giving them fish, have understood that they can still fish. They have it under control for their good, for the government-plin and the sweet coconut madam. The reality, I have not developed my potential for conversation either, and I feel that it is a strong reason to explore and give opinions as far as the paper and your help allow, breaking down any connection, whether individual, collective, personal, or impulsive.

Guilty by association, and if the Crazy Hill had sold me the airplane, I would swear the environment and the reasons to converge in the old park, the Mister Einstein was not wrong. Imagination, and since then, we wondered with common sense and evidence. From there it depends on to raise the level of the ball game through expansion. It is worth incurring risks, the interference to the daily struggle of the game can be affected in game and business. In anticipating expansion, some streams of ancestry will give interest. Reality presents us, among history, the current barbaric production in the golden age is governed as a narrative of secret wars for control. In the past, interest in control led the day of resentments, invaluable mistakes as lessons to perfection well known to the eminent. However, profit turned disaster into comfort, and everything turned into win-win moments. The time has arrived where you reveal those lessons and apply them to the collaborative method. Believe it or not, the actions of distributing the booty equitable to the productive effort surpasses any other current before the push of the day. Creativity in bringing the game to the armchair and super wide screen? How many shoes did we sell? Do we care about remodeling stadiums, we would say, uniform around 42,000 seats? The figure comes from thinking of the minimum to continue in position to go back to the postseason.

And if the idea returns the debate that broadening will result in a salary cap? It is not noted, by the incredible control in the nature of the business, and the distribution of wealth follows the flow of capitalism. Also, already the Association has under iron the benefits of the players and with the plan up their sleeve. Salary caps can not be subject to evaluation. The spectrum of the business and the existing balance in the scale of organizational power does not allow shaking the amounts achieved with much sweat and struggle. The income distribution system is considered a salary cap, but the least harmful. It is soft and manageable and is responsible for the current balance. And what of the current boom? The ways to invest and earn money are versatile. No one wants to talk about interrupting a warm and substantial remuneration for playing ball in capitalist territory.

Mike Ozanian, in Forbes magazine, states that average income and operating income (earnings before interest, taxes, depreciation and amortization) for the 30 MLB teams were over $ 315 million and $ 29 million, respectively, in the 2017 season Revenues increased 4.7% compared to 2016, mainly due to more television, seats and luxury boxes and sponsorship money. Meanwhile, operating revenues fell 17% mainly due to higher spending on marketing, player development and analytics. The factual in the reference, in service to the honor of not tracing the remote, before maneuvering tactics in the unpublished segments, checks the current condition. We already said it is the effect of the use of the contraption in the field and on the stands and sell and get the fans away from the stadium see the pod by digital devices. Win-win situations are the norm.

Among the current, capitalism provides no other way to redirect employment versus pay, but maintain control, streamline leadership and the powers of studies, as well as the unique human knowledge and the broad perspective of the experts inside. But where does the money go to pay for $8 hotdogs and beer? We are sure a lot today has changed. If there was no barbarous prosperity, it was not for the support of the fanatics and the business chain weaving every second while you read and you are passionate about understanding the fold where the sting in the persuasive is collected. To dominate the game and its chains of business has been, for the well-off, the picture seeing the same success with the same curiosity, and the operators of "front office" in all the franchises deserve credit for keeping the cord of business tempered and trained in the constant work between distribution agreements. Success with the luxury of sports is highly predictable because it is specialized. We are attracted to accept preference for the collective, the avid for profitability to share the coffers. What if in decade investors receive the deferred slice with interest? In additional suggestion to the rational optimism in mutual cooperation and shared decision-the revenues, the route and the distribution of utilities to many sources is part of the secret in the wars of power. This is history, now prosperity rules—the old Bobby Bonilla retirement story.

Today prestige concentrates on cooperation. Those battles for dominance almost throw the game by the cliff. To the contemporary premium, the machinery to make money enriches everyone. According to the references intercalan the advance of gains flowing to all, we begin to imagine those who take the wool. The attitudes and fortitudes of sharing wealth have turned to the positive with the possibility of undertaking a greater agenda. Surely obvious, those with short imagination will say it's not worth concentrating on the initiative. The risk is worth using the same control that almost derails the train of wealth. No initiative separates from the contest. 162 games will remain the norm. Arriving and winning the

World Series is another type of war of powers putting pressure to follow without many changes in the structure. You arrive if you do not suffer scratches, if the list of injured does not slow you down. Keeping the current contest according to the rules and the summer manual in hope the fall teach smell more tickets for the effort of equipment and improvement of the functions. We would have to analyze what makes the postseason intense, for example, and develop energy accordingly. First, we understand that drastic changes are not easy in this world of competition, of luxury, between risks, and second, opportunities require dynamics.

That, without leaving precious anecdotes on the outside, the risk is another dimension for another dissertation with equally deep angles, in each act of reenginization. About the MLB reorganization, too high before placing the required level of resources. No one wants to get rid of playing more games against them within the geographical division, the subject of contracts and salaries is kept secret between agents of players and general managers. There is even the excuse that you should not expunge situations that may affect the tradition. But the idea of reorganizing, in the end, can generate initiatives so that future generations do not have to absorb the debt for the construction of new stadiums.

At the MLB level, it must be like eating a peanut, because at that level analytics is of caliber to complete the play. MLB possesses high octane in human analytical constitution and that inspired by tradition and the splicing of the game development manual, technology and in-game and business activities. The habit that emanates, as in the game, is perfection. We were not going to use evasive vocabulary. We were going to try straight ahead that soccer went partying. In the long run, victim of chance. What if the proposal hits? Although the strange thing began for another cycle to the size of "protected forum", although we knew that baseball's magnates don't want to rock the cradle of an absolutely profitable composition and disposition. Beyond imagination, you do not need additional awareness to realize it. Growing additional clubs is the safe and feasible way to enlarge baseball. And there is no exact way to perceive it. It is not necessary to include the concept of the academy as part of the subscriptions to the minor leagues. Suppose that everyone wants decent contenders, increased profits, and be willing to get out of the fairy tale by building new stadiums. Consider the cost for fans who pay to support the game we love, and you can not hear "we are moving the franchise." It matters better an investment for all, in the end everyone would be owners of expansion. Money does matter, and the favorable events surface by the minutes.

Really? Is the decade for expansion around the corner?

*"In 1961, Tony Oliva, three times batting champion was re-
leased by the Minnesota Twins on the first day of spring training after signing for an obscene $200. The Twins did not think
Tony could hit. "*

~ Marcos Bretón & José Luis Villegas
Away Games: The life and times of a latin baseball player

It doesn't have to be a guava if you tell your story your
own way, without surprising anyone, it turned out to
be the beautiful answer from Alma, the mother of information in Saigón Chiquita. Prepare several unknowns
on paper and review them often, had suggested yesterday an eighth grader in Escuela de Puerto Rico. Since
then, I understood that the children of the School of
Puerto Rico are awesome to the hyperbole of wanting to
play, enjoying winning for the satisfaction of the manager, or for sure the teacher's ear jerk has the homework
being below grade. I instantly knew this generation X, Y,
or whatever believed in soccer. They were quite at-
tracted to the depth of baseball as the visit implied, while
several teachers and administrators sat around the room.

Elmer Giralt was the chief moderator in that instance.
To enter Panama's Department of Education and being
welcomed so warmly is not easy but served as punchline.
The construction guild was on strike closing streets, but
the school faculty picked the best young minds to gives
us their perspective. As we entered the building with our
charts, we looked at the blackboard. In particular, the

students at the School of Puerto Rico surprised us by the back door. In wide letters the singularity of baseball: 2019-2030. Imagine 2019 is to think about it and call a meeting. Perhaps, during Baseball Winter Meetings, December 8-12, 2019, in San Diego. An opportunity to join baseball executives and staff, media, exhibitors and job seekers from around the world to discuss innovative industry trends and ideas and exchange best practices.

It's true, the purpose of memory is futuristic and don't allow too much future to get by. We've being hoping to decipher the timeline. Whenever you need support giving balance to the thing put an imaginative tone into it but beware of Branch Rickey. Surely, he'll make you believe the lefty behind the barn does have arm pain or problems with the curve. Pay enough attention to the situation, suddenly, in which we had gotten into. How could it happen? The reason to choose mentoring and in every instance created an air about the importance of unconventional themes in the midst of a regular curriculum break. The ten-year agenda arose from that memory, because behind the great ideas shines some kind of value adjustable to a future benefit. Time to dress Little Red Riding Hood to her perfect size.

From that morning on, assuming the agenda as sensible, coming to building an independent but adjustable product advancement, important to get rid of the status quo. Despite the status quo carries a reason inside, as well as what concerns the portentous to preserve welfare, the secret waits in between key organizational elements. Appreciating the functions and results from the pillars of baseball is something interesting to mark on the map that the beams supporting the sport hone on value in case you'll have to sell or relocate the franchise. Unless you even attempt against a system in high range product of engendered goals. Since 1922, baseball is exempted from antitrust practices and categories, just in case the detractors argue it will be robbery. The antitrust benefit is probably the stone with uncomfortable weight, which in the contemporary is almost nil until the value is mortgaged and perhaps, associate use of value is another good vibe in the current design of strategies hoping for a unified decision. Before modifying the game and its banking and resources to play and win, the value in the chain interlacing the sport is the driver of profitability not exactly quantified, but multilateral. Tell me something else nobody knows. MLB tops the list with powerful and lucrative franchises. There is great leverage in television transmission contracts. The exclusive rights are sold, but the owners of the teams have great participation. Each game generates income rights, membership fees and advertising. From a good pull of earlobe, one thing was clear amidst intrigue. It's time. We were not weaving simple things either. We assume moderating the pupils on the hill and as a goal, the project always called for focus on sectors away from the sport. Did the boys act in favor of watching Baseball's growth, or did they put their granite of vision, even if it was Trojan illusion? In the end, we discovered they were eager to express the merit sport is given its place. They put us in the hands of the reference with everything and the welts on the feet by the march in the alleys and alleys of Pueblo Nuevo to go up to the little school. Asking the citizens who believe, and many indicated not only the Major Leagues should ride the Trojan Horse, but all business stratum with room to grow. A man asked, can this be developed in basketball? I answered the idea does not apply to the competition, until MLB goes ahead, and others do not want to continue below.

It would be necessary to focus applying memory to the survival of tomorrow. Without placing a tradition on the science of curiosity, putting an eagerness into it and leaving whatever it was, it gives you something to think about. When trying to design the future, a varied level of realism must be deployed, intertwining the wide range of economic, political and social factors. If you handle and surpass unexpected conditions, there would be reason to call a meeting and unleash the process with unique curiosity. Establishing nine farm subscriptions for each expansion franchise requires depth of resources, mainly capital and playing talent. That's why the common sense of cooperation is the surprise mode. The owners of stadiums, in a consortium, could pay for stadium remodeling to accommodate expansion at the Major level. Expansion does not need the unnecessary cost in new stadiums. Except when you run into the situation in Las Vegas. The first earth shovel for the construction of Las Vegas Park, stadium with capacity for 10,000 fans, has already been removed, and the cost is already $ 150 million. The old Cashman Field, home of the 51's in the Pacific Coast League, deteriorated, and as long as there is a need to maintain the triple A franchise in Las Vegas, it is also difficult to establish Senior team. In San Antonio, in 1919 the Missions continue playing in the Nelson Wolff Municipal Stadium, but with transfer from the Texas League (AA) to the Pacific Coast League (AAA). Definitely great challenges, because there are already arrangements of stay of minor teams, but not impossible reformatting if those of the elite begin to discuss expansion.

On the farm, fragrances do not lack to learn discipline and refinement of character. Mastering the chair to play up involves a lot of learning, and much of the talent is lost while those pre-eminent who are now not part of the dream of reaching the top fade into society. If we promise to design an academic program to develop baseball, it would not be the precise signal to the potential of the expert pillar penetrating the municipality. Output, similar to exposing the secret method of playing in coupling. In seguidilla, the reception of a franchise means hope for the people raised by the terrible evils lurking home weaknesses and social chaos that does not take prisoners. As relentless as it sounds, empowering the great values at the MLB pillars urges us to see not only capital, but also the wealth-creating spectrum. The legacy of expansion in other regions and times speaks for itself. And it was not until 1998 that the Arizona Diamondbacks and Tampa Devil Rays emerged, the latest on the avenue. Until then, we all know the norm of expanding two teams at a time, and decades have passed, and participation has not increased. Perhaps we suggest taking a decision too narrow considering the narrative of urgency as for impact if you walk in persuasive ideas and perspectives with no plan to avoid the repercussions. The last question would be to realign the teams in the leagues, make the Designated Hitter uniform, convert the Wild Card to a series of five games, and double the number of contenders to 16 in the postseason.

At the level of other important pillars and with scope never discard the power of the Hall of Fame, the Players Association, the Scouting Bureau, and SABR. As the Society for American Baseball Research, SABR has a lot of scope and can assist towards much-needed changes. There is room to visualize how much power would be delegated to the Expansion Management Agency. Luckily three quarters of the process are already frozen in the data servers, and by the harmony displayed, even the mundane aspects of the obsession that we call hardball would be in agreement if it brings collective benefit. How about an analytical opinion of Baseball Prospectus and the potential of MLBAM to be the expansion manager? Shall Baseball hands over the franchise keys, the alliance with Major League Advanced Media, the large contract that has stabilized everything relevant to net profits has been the result of such a wise strategy, and it'd be reasonable to look into her investment reach. We've been looking in the wrong places. BAM made a contract at a higher level, and separate contracts with all the franchises. The return on investment has been healthy. For the year 2017, the brand value of MLBAM was $2.4 billion, that's why we're not sipping through a punched straw.

Baseball needs a timeline or about ten years, or figurable, cutting the ribbon ahead, if the goal is 40 clubs. You can't look for advise the whole move in so few pages, but if you can swear with BAM at the helm, we'd be confident. Unless with MLBAM in charge of the core penetrating the uneasy, new ways to manage franchises of expansion from Baseball's leadership. Imagine the financial power of BAM makes him the choice candidate and his results make you think it all meshes in that any imbalance be respected, everything reflects in delegating the key pieces to the elite of results. Without triggering the reserve cavalry too early.

Welcome to the era of business, times of strength for roads, bridges and alternate roads. Instigate to know if there is mining in the west for exploitation. How would the enormous population of Montreal exploit the opportunity not to lose the franchise again? We do not know, but chemistry of groups of course, that for those who have had the privilege of playing ball, this is the difficult space that we do not recommend if you do not want to get involved in a game with intensity and a lot to lose.

The tank of thought resides within, between the branches that maintain the sport in optimum splendor with the grace of the usual judicious consensus. In addition, a new negotiation model can change the game forever, although here we delegate to the insiders the actual confection based on this simulation. The good practice of thinking about the back key in cooperation would be a plausible initiative to always continue to support the objectives of mastering the game in its entirety. Baseball is a society played as a game, and probably the main reason to grow for the benefit of all. There is no problem of what this idea may fit in individual opinions or in what dump land. The importance lies in the fact that the evolution of the baseball economy will finally end in a new model. There are hints the geographical replenishment would require a separate plan. Of course, a series of plans, each one his own. As we move into the CBA (Collective Bargaining Agreement) 2017-2021 agreements, who would not be interested in results.

Who would not be expanding the vision about the return of Montreal? Would we be interested in a highly competitive franchise in Oklahoma? Maybe you're interested in visiting the Riverwalk to see the San Antonio Broncos look for a slot in the postseason. If so, the conquest of the west has already formulated its own opinions. We are generating a brainstorm of useful ideas.

Talking about markets and money in large numbers tend to blur the possibility of success. One thing leads to another. In the end, what is worth to the market, although researching the feeling amongst fans it ought to make us a voice to like, dislike and look at the lead compartments. Get their feeling with forward feeling you may have the same, as Baseball's pillars hold strong. And what about contemporary alliances to make the leap? What if instead of skull we break the pot in the direction of creating function policies with the use of historical context. You have to do your own work in a communication path, conflicts and labor battles. The already established control systems can act as pillars to a more condensed exercise. From the formidable of the alliances, it is sought to distribute the resources in equanimity, which has been the current strength. Then we ponder what would have happened if the players had not resorted to the unionist strategy to level their benefits before a profession that takes away a large portion of your family and personal life. In fact, to ponder all these knots is to verify the individual result or in compartments that bring and take the game to the national and international level. But it is not until we form an image of breaking down the functional "make-up" of the department and apply creativity to it, sometimes in an extreme scenario.

What is clear is that there is no precise way to capture ink to the baseball game. But you can think free about the Baseball's organizational record suspected decoration of working smart, not hard. Do you remember the birth of the National League, with Ban Johnson creating the American League, since Magistrate Kennesaw 'Mountain' Landis in 1922 decreed the monopoly advantage? In 1979 the umpires earned under $40 thousand for calling 170 games—now, the minimum salary of an arbitrator is near or over $200K (plus some benefits), and experienced veteran players can earn 500 plus per season. The rest is history, prosperity is revolutionary.

No next-door big competitor matches the diverse marketing around the qualities of Baseball. On the stage of resources has no shortage of talent. People that man these types of marketing daredevils also know that the battlefield calls for playing with depth. No manager would ask for less. Symbolically and reserved, as the themes drive what you want to communicate, the most difficult thing is to measure the resources and that the clubs share them. Of course, the commitment emanates from the effort and the utility of the assets if fortune must be maintained and extended. Since inside there is absolute understanding of the game and its resources. The broken-record sound of collaboration grasps the strategy and convert luck to success and does not turn back. Smooth in the new geographical realm. Assumptions and trying to adopt our own internal sketch. Assume that to perform superior, quality has to do with maintaining the leadership capable of gathering the winning depth.

In the support of leagues under expansion there is no other way. Reaching reality to ensure balance, to follow rivalries and continue to support to create better lives, never to disassociate from the beneficial part of the game to the community and focus on the designs of capitalism. The ones that are effective. The fabric targets on the assumption that wealth is revolutionary. Assuming the name of the game remains potential to attract interest, that dynamism is profitable for those inclined to the sporting future. We also stand to discuss the continuity of competitive balance finding better agendas and methods to bring the game to the community, and important that the market region accepts and supports the professional clubs. Maybe at the next meeting on the hill of intrigue we can sketch the internal blueprint.

8 |
With beaks and spurs

"I love baseball with passion. The guys and the game, and the challenge to describe things. The only thing I hate—and I know you have to be realistic and pay the bills—is loneliness on the road."

~ Vin Scully
Dodgers Commentator and baseball chronicler

The rest is history and the central desire is to play ball to another level. The voice reference points to the real. In January 2016, Commissioner Robert Manfred indicated that the National League could adopt the Designated Hitter for the 2017 season through the latest collective bargaining agreement. However, he later retracted his statement not to see DH in the National League for the time being. How trivial is the designated hitter?

The morning at the start of the Winter Meetings in Buena Vista I had a dream about how safe it would be in a few years. The first to sign for ofer $400 million is a reality. Our fantasy side turned the time machine to 1973. As in the afternoons of urban "stickball". The bat, broomstick, in a thick frame, elongated to cover the swing area, sometimes too wild. And it's not with racket ball if I tell you, it's fallacy the need to pay more by signing a free caliber agent to abuse the DH on the batting list. It's the greatest an illusion. Today it is more profitable to have hitters with high on-base average in the lineup. The Designee does not provide long-term power to the manager. The preparation of the alignment falls in the domain of how the Director has the depth, the not easy in the goals of the team. Assimilating that anyone who is sparking with the bat can assume the role anywhere in the string, but under the conscience of that authority as director. Imagining the even DH in both leagues is a return of impact. There is no need to expand on the safety of turning the balance in favor of hitting, with pitching around 60 percent of the game and sometimes scoring a run is impossible. Fans want to see liners in the gap to fly on the basepaths, longing for the hook-slide, that of Roberto Clemente—legs open, body eluding touch of the glove. Giving 130 percent for the team.

Very difficult to leave the DH outside. Big Papi owns a lot of firewood as designated hitter. Equally, you never discard use of the seventh sense in the reason the executive should delegate the matter to those responsible on the side of the game. It can be sorted out with an electorate, a majority among all the players, and managers and coaches. A vote to see if the National League adopts the Designated Hitter, and additional chance to give more credit to Edgar Martinez as a deadly hitter, only visualizes Edgar covered the area of blows with his bat Rawlings Pro Blonde quite frequent for extra bases. The free agents of the future may have a part-time job, but it is not worth discarding reality. In the cave of the Majors, it is true, play in the box and own bat to picture of Manny Ramirez indicates ponderar free will to hear the voice of the reputed and their anecdotes. We look for something to come out from inside, taking advantage of the return to the origin.

On January 11, 1973, Charley Finley and other owners of the American League had chosen a majority by vote of 8-4 to introduce the designated hitter. Pilot plan for three years, and it's been alive since. On 6 April1973 it was sunny but a little cold at 55 degrees Fahrenheit in Fenway Park. The annals of history mark that afternoon as the day that Eddie Kasko was a leader of Boston. The Red Sox with local advantage, however, Manager Kasko handed his lineup to Frank Umont, referee assigned behind the plate:

BOSTON RED SOX
1 Tommy Harper LF
2 Luis Aparicio SS
3 Carl Yastrzemski IB
4 Reggie Smith CF
5 Orlando Cepeda DH
6 Rico Petrocelli 3B
7 Carlton Fisk C
8 Doug Griffin 2B
9 Dwight Evans RF
Luis Tiant P

The Yankees visited their rival in the American League. Careful not to let it fly, as the winds blew at 20 miles per hour, Umont circulated the list for verification. First, Ralph Houk, the Yankees manager, followed by the bases crew; Don Denkinger, Merle Anthony and Bill Deegan, whom all nodded, and Houk handed the Yankee lineup, previously having scored Ron Blomberg batting sixth as Designated Hitter.

NEW YORK YANKEES
1 Horace Clarke 2B
2 Roy White LF
3 Matty Alou RF
4 Bobby Murcer CF

5 Graig Nettles 3B
6 Ron Blomberg DH
7 Felipe Alou 1B
8 Thurman Munson C
9 Gene Michael SS
Mel Stottlemyre P

The group repeated the ritual and Peruchín Cepeda was officially the first DH in the American League. Ron Blomberg was the first to complete a turn at bat as DH, and before 32,882 fans, Blomberg in four at bats hit a single and received a free ticket. Cepeda went hitless in six turns. Ever since, there is a venerable tradition divided between leagues. Several studies have been done to see if the designated hitter causes better production in the American League. The organization "Fangraphs" found that by measuring Isolated Power (ISO) (batting for extra bases) the American League had more production runs from 1973 to 2000. The National League, even without the use of DH, has been gaining ground in batting outside of the park at a distance and frequent. We assume it is the weighty category as scoring runs is the most important approach in winning. What if I say we believe is a fallacy the need to pay more by signing a caliber free agent to abuse with nine hitters in the batting order. It's another illusion. In baseball, it's more profitable to have hitters in the lineup with high on-base percentage. Look at the incipient dispararaty some attribute to tradition onto the strategy to play. The DH does provide long-reach to the manager. The director's desire has depth—guessing as the winning element—understanding and imagining that in a simple initial step to establish uniformity in the DH ought to be a return to the outcomes of impact—as it's just we've just maintained waste of common sense.

As time passed, the designated hitter rule has ended giving American League managers multiple strategic options to establish their team's line-up: they can rotate DH's role among part-time players, or they can use a batter designated full time against all pitchers. It also allows them to give days of rest to offensive or injured players the opportunity to hit without exposing them to the aggravation of injuries while playing defense. The DH offers both managers to enter the domain of questioning. Do you need to produce runs? And what of the allowed ones? That is why the game has remained in eternal balance with the intricate. Already the studies have been done, internal and commercial. Tons of data, while the forceful comes to light. DH is popular in many leagues. A good manager visualizes his batting lineup according to his strategy against the opposing pitcher. In that brief lapse the power to hit for outside can rest in the middle, the small ball may be in play, or simply, the assumption that a third bat will drive more runs by hitting third behind two with high average in base. Lately we see power hitters in lines one and two. That leads us to think that the higher in the lineup, the more turns to the batter's box to guarantee more runs scored.

The uniform DH is another opportunity hidden from view. Even without the use of it, it has been gaining ground in batting power, distance and frequency although evidence points that the offensive in the National League is rising. Keeping the DH uniformly brings benefits. Older players with intact batting skills, either power or going into base, pose greater challenges to defense stands. Today the science of bringing runs to home is important. People like the sound of the bat. A greater benefit would be to keep the pitchers focused on their pitching area—less chance of injury—and managers can use the depth of the bench in other instances as in extra innings.

Not so fast, it'd be imperative putting a premium on a decision on the Designated Hitter. Players, coaches and managers could decide on wiping out of embracing the DH uniformly in an electoral forum. It all may seem like a harmless activity for the delight of functional managers who spend too long facing risks while allocating funds and staff to projects driven on forecast. Keeping the DH uniformly brings benefits. Older players with intact hitting abilities, whether is hammer or contact relieve a pitching staff too concentrated on pitching and defense fundamentals. Today the science of not allowing the opposition to score is premium.

The fallacy you need to pay more to have a big free agent as DH is just an illusion. The team payroll is more intrinsic to know the details, as the composition of the financial sheets in MLB is best understood inside. From the fan perspective, many crossing influences take effect. Before any decision on the DH, the drive for progress is the determinant that trumps the parts in tradition one can't get rid of. One thing I can guess right: MLB has vested interests in drive of value with a sense of purpose beyond just making money. So many requisites in the way. None is impossible, very difficult to leave the DH on the outside. Equally, you never discard use of the seventh sense by fanning intensity in the reason the National League executive should delegate the matter to those responsible on the side of the game. Baseball players, coaches, coaches, managers and the Chief Baseball Officers of all the clubs. The electoral tournament, in most, would discover the Designated Hitter is a force to the markets to advance more opportunities into the explosion of talent rigged by lots of batting practice.

Unifying the fabric: utility and experience

"Every day in the park, there is the potential for joy—a game-winning hit, a game-saving catch, a game-ending strikeout. The route to that joy is far less understood."

~ Barry Svrluga
The Grind: Inside Baseball's Endless Season

In 2019, in conjunction with the preparation of expansion stadiums, there is room for obviously extreme changes. Knock down the East, Central and West divisions in both leagues, and double 16 teams in the postseason - and convert the wild card game to five-game series.

Our last secret weapon turned out to be the investigation of the path of organized baseball and the tracking of its interests and searches for the improvement of athletic performance. Things that would not be put in text to its fullness but allow the descriptive reveal the power of intuition to the truth of the data. Given the unusual of having a tool to be unified, but immovable by its frontier of responsibility and excuses to continue reclining on the area of tranquility. The scenario of the future brings the image of fighting in alliance. What better the alliance that exists in. The domains with merit for the dense prosperity. The same general now can place in his theater that a frontal attack is executed when you are in the best disposition of resources. The name of the initiative remains the management of the control topology, whatever that means, MLB has that pig chained for Easter parties, and few in the corporate universe can teach how to turn it into cracklings.

We do not need to modify much on the advance plan for expansion unifying forces. It depends, if the solution has already made amends. We would answer that during the synthesis by comparing the strength of the elements to the challenge. After questioning, this should not be dangerous to common goals.

Questioning control in baseball brings us to the Grand Paradigm (purpose) to lead interest in the game, competitive equality, win money and distribute it, and have the honor of contributing to society. Then we face the same direction for comparative purposes (in other analytical circles and scientific studies), because now in the present the important thing is to understand that comparing is also the back key, and finally we place the corners of the baseball total and outside the sphere of the dynamics with edges for thickness sandpaper. While upscaling the game requires achieving balance in all the objectives, the road map would not be better if it shaked the growing magneto of the postseason, in search in better interest for the game, competitive balance and benefits to the collective.

It's enough. Baseball has in hand the concepts of utility and experience before the impact facts playing in the diamond and with the economy. Putting the central point of forecasting the best unified management formulating processes and assumptions, there is the possibility of structural changes. How much would it affect the resources? The resources are larger pieces that compared with the total scope, could support the impetus in the mother of the investments. Luckily, baseball dominates that picture. In proper perspective, Expansión 2018-2026 depends on a unifying process of influence, professionalism to advance the legacy of the summer pastime.

And with this we figure the rest is full conversation in conflicting opinions, equally comparing the perspective depends on whether from within or from our level here in the now. Imagine that the route with less risk is to develop the scheme from within. You avoid unnecessary expenses and time in counseling. The advisors reside inside. And they are usually the operational wedges in challenges without turning back. Any agenda does not have other than to look for balance in the Great Paradigm. And while in the subject there is always the optimum of putting a level of possibility (secondary agenda). Between assuming that it is possible to expand to a diagram of six major franchises in ten years in the need to establish farm franchises, which looks imposing. Here we begin on how to apply influence, professionalism and the interest of returning to the social origin are imperative in any agenda on product advancement. On that the perspectives depend. And I began to ponder the diagram of the project, leaving us the solution to the solution that in other areas are attached to the response from the back door. Assume we have penetrated a simulation with nuances of placing the incompatible in the order of cooperation to complete the task since challenge has stepped within range.

No matter the situation, someone will think that MLB has anti-monopoly advantages. First you have to consider baseball as a sport is an intrinsic matrix of 30 different business models with 30 different philosophies that play in 30 stadiums, none built the same. Clubs mark their products in large and small markets, while other significant elements of success include the farm system, roster of players, key external interests, solid perspectives and execution of operations and strategies to win. No less important, the biggest national and international hobby is transformed into a variety of flavors: those with traditional perspectives, those of the modern method learned to assimilate the game, those that favor the route and behavior in the role of entertainment, and the notorious ones dedicated to hate, to misinformation and everything that opposes proven success. The first strategic order is assuming a central perspective that considers the capacities and avoids that what is not aligned does not interfere. Part of the scenario is to scratch the alignment and in a plaster in some wall or corner of the "dugout" for higher analytics. It is better, while the morning sun inspires the antagonistic or unified order in solution to the diagram. It helps us to evaluate the machinery of thoughts, free and optional. Arriving at the rear solution does not imply that we do not share the same perspective in time, space and strategic order. A lot of talk is not appropriate either. Everything is related to your abilities and what you can control. Make your own sense of working with what there is. Then you ask for the resources for the assignment.

Welcome to the order of the curious. The main leagues can compare with each other and verify how good regulations create effectiveness and efficiency of functions at all levels. Nowadays the owners enjoy a better relationship with the Association. Some may remain dissatisfied with the results of the luxury tax, without forgetting that everyone is doing good in pursuit of collective actions for the benefit of many. Ultimately, it boils down to the excellence in which MLB has organized asset management in a systematic and scientific manner. At the other end of the torch, baseball knows how to place a complex interrelation of its components and resources. Perhaps the greatest search can reveal the essentially competitive nature has raised cooperative instincts making reconfiguration easier through agreements. The cooperative mode is the norm. For the lover of freedom of thought, Baseball's historic journey appears nothing less than due to strength in coherence. That old tradition is bathed in wealth and assumes that heritage is the dress of its colors buried in anecdotes and fascinating little-known facts and even the intangible as stadiums, internal battles between traditionalists and modernists, experts, lobbying and interests, and strategies of marketing to the spectrum of entertainment and exploitation of perfor-mance and fame. With the aim of placing the idea, at the end of the day the own interests are compatible with the mutual help. One of my favorite writers is Matt Ridley. He said that tit-for-tat means exchange of similar favors at different times, and anthropologists refer to reciprocity as the virtue that chance provides a temporary benefit to other needs. The opportunity pays the debt, we remem-ber the good intention, generosity, social recognition and public spirit are mixed. It is worth exploring the de-bate in reciprocity. Precisely central is the art of reci-procity in the exchange of wealth, Seniors are financially self-sufficient as they evolved as part of the nature of baseball on both sides, game, and business. In identity forged in two leagues and there were great threats to such a structure. In a field, negotiation is queen. Uniting resources consolidates power in the area of sharing the burden of goods and services to a fair division of benefits.

It means then, money is motivating for the knowledge of entrepreneurship in all branches of sport, marketing focus under the essence of capitalism. In ref-erence, the background words are Mathew Futterman in Players: The Story of Sports and Money, and the Vision-aries Who Fought to Create a Revolution. The executives in charge fought battles against the athletes, the fall in those battles, and the revolution created the giant in sports being the arc of this story. It is an attempt to under-stand how we arrived at the place of extravagance with high production, always commercialized.

What has been the wool record card produced by the intensity of the postseason? But how much does the expansion cost? They do not require answers out of context. The way we do it so that the intense benefits reach the franchises of expansion is just another idea of lightning to weave avenues and paths with risks, but suitable for the application of controls. In sports, agreeing the ingredients and giving adequate resources is parallel to the science of competing. Then it would be possible to establish an illustrator plan with the principles of guiding us through the sources of information and numbers. Investigating and interpolating experiences I came across Game Changers, a fabulous book by George Castle. It provides a number of examples, such as the advent of free agency, television, night games and arbitration. According to Castle, baseball and television need each other to survive. Opposed to the 50s when the television ball originated, today transmissions are a source cornucopia in competition-local stations such as FOX, ESPN, TBS and MLB Network among the infinity of chains. Welcome to the list of allies with enough economic influence to jointly deploy the proposal. On the topology of control through rational optimism and common sense there is much to talk about. Seeking someone with influence to notice it through assertions and moving facts full of surprise and intrigue. Facts needing to look for the fifth leg to the cat, and perhaps on this trip the game is still underestimated. Its past events correlate with the contemporary status of the power of influence to enhance prosperity in broad spheres of the community. It is easy to underestimate the objectives of wealth beyond the municipality and the business network and the altruistic work required. Anyone who appreciates sport will in part believe in favor of improving, it means taking the political entry while adhering to the social virtue in the golden rule is to concentrate on the current level of power and its effects, and never underestimate who is going to constitute a formidable opposition.

We are quite sure that all the cadres and segments in the baseball spectrum are responsible for the enormous prosperity and confidence placed in trying to tame the beast of the unknown. Welcome to the era of business, of the fortress of roads, bridges and alternative roads. It instigates us to know if there in the west, by Utah there's mining and plenty a sun to exploit good old field day.

10 |
Influence

"I have crossed the infinite layers negotiating horses and creating agreements, delivery and intrigue, which govern the sports industry and whatever. I know the intimacy of becoming familiar with the rules and risks that dominate the world of power and influence."

~ *Jerry Colángelo with Len Sherman*
How You Play the Game: Lessons for Life from the Billion-Dollar Business of Sports

On the other side of the Rio Mataznillo wall there is a house that fascinates you with solid opinions. It's a Wednesday and Oliver wakes up early, goes to the bathroom, tells Alma to pull the chain. The blond boy now is not the same "superstar" of Team Puerto Rico. Nor are the tennis that he sponsors to solve prosperity before being a free agent - he is the operator of a much more refined marvel. Alma is not the cute girl who accompanies him whenever he tweets or publishes social media life outside the diamond.

I knocked on the door and Elmer offered me a caffeine refill. He had been the first to arrive in Panama, by the end of the 70s. He brought us a C-30 from Charleston Air Force Base. The jungle below, the view of the Pacific Ocean projected me back not only to Falcon's lampoons, the Green Lantern and the Wonder Woman. With the dense verdure came the desire to repatriate my experiences in baseball, which had freed me from inconveniences in the unusual streets of Chicago. Elmer knew a lot about that.

Elmer Giralt, a native of the Villa del Capitán Correa, a tremendous mentor. He had met him in charge of "Field Inquiry", the community newspaper of Humboldt Park in the city of the winds. It was the time when Jerry Morales was patrolling the central forest at Wrigley Field, and the day we saw Roberto Clemente hit a line-drive homer like a bullet outside the stadium. It was against Ferguson Jenkins, his 240th career dinger, and sixth against Jenkins. Ah yes, the afternoon all the Cubs fans gave Clemente a standing ovation.

An important fact, returning the sequel good old memories of my best mentors, because this is also on how great mentors play second base, well, all positions like a select few among my teachers, counselors and motivators. Jumping the border of the moment would depend on a meeting to weave the historical and the trivial. We went to the terrace next to the Río Mataznillo cinder-block wall and at first, I didn't show my deep concerns, but it had nothing to do with persuasive storytelling, the next to best admiration next to baseball. It's not another fact that unified effort is always the key to commitment.

My concerns were parallel to the tricks of politicians—turf that if you don't judge yor bare-foot stepping the wet stones beneath, your tail gets wet crossing the riverbed. As to what the fans and the persuasive recipients could make of it? Expansion to 36 is the central framework that carries great burden; thus, no interference trumps it can be shaped alright. At this and the next pages we won't try nothing spectacular or do anything additional but let the vast experience of those gathered around the oval table dictate the best of their repertoire. Advising the aim to be smart with the mental notes about the opposers and their probable reasons. Because time is still upon us, from that instant, an electronic notice penetrating the headphones:

Residente: Hey, check something with Alma. I need the projection of the value of the Expos

Oliver: but already? why so sudden? The franchise is not for sale. Wouldn't the meeting attendees defer profits to tie taxes? For ten years, they said. What does BAM say?

Residente: It's not saying anything, and I need you to find out. We are looking at the sponsorships, marketing, the exact # of talent in the local economy and the BAM report card.

Oliver: Does BAM have problems managing the municipality in Montreal?

Residente: Something. It is nothing serious, it is serious that there is an initiative to manipulate the current exposure of the Expos

Oliver: Wait a second ... the franchise has low value. Is it prudent? I will get it done in five. While you can lighten up Alma over Tijuana.

Residente: Enlighten her and tell her that Tijuana will be considered for the 2nd leg beginning in 2027.

The line went dead. Alma passed him another call. The blonde boy adjusted the unit behind the ear, I do not know who might be on the other end but must've been someone with influence urging to add his grain of salt. I imagined it could be Mister Robert Bowman BAM's CEEO. I knew the conversation was directed to determine the number of seats; those that are rented; and the luxury boxes to exploit thick bills requires that the expansion stadium be hung at the top of the clubs with a miserable chance to enter the "playoffs". BAM, in charge of managing the expansion clubs, would concentrate effort on adapting five or six thousand seats on the minimum reality of 36-thousand seating capacity of the current small markets. And what if the new franchises demand resources to drive the tournament in the fall. The nonverbal message warned me that I had come to the indicated barracks, and while it seemed that the executives made the big move with BAM in command, the narrative of the Magnificos would not even be believed by the brigade of stray cats that invaded Saigón Chiquita and whe willingness of the city major in restraining trash pickup to every two weeks. The air was foul. I had made too much effort and had the helmet blowing smoke—I recognize—for doing the difficult thing with the right index finger, and not for emphasis of carrying the battle to be persuaded. That's why I visited my old friends. I saw myself climbing the stairs, entering the bedroom on the right. Direct to the little room of dwarves and cockroaches for an "energy" recharge, this time in the voice of the reference so that they do not tell me stories. I could not believe in that tiny space between the variety of literature was "Circling the Bases: Essays on the Challenges and Prospects of the Sports Industry", by Andrew Zimbalist.

The conference room was in the bedroom with the perpendicular window and an imposing and appreciable view of the 1A street. Inside, the voice of the reference with its pages open to dialogue. I pulled the gravity magnet book on the floor, curled my aching spine out of the square hole. I felt page 47, part of 3: Competitive Balance: Leveling the Playing Field. Master Zimbalist details that in the early 1990s the escalation of the monetary attractiveness of franchises limits the power of ownership. It says only the rich to the extraordinary or corporations, who already enjoy ownership in media entities, and own businesses connected to baseball. The curious thing about the connection is his declaration that the new owners value their players not outside the production in the field, but towards the performance in their media networks and their investments. The dream of those interested in the business is parallel to the brutality of telling the narrative in order to please the majority. It includes not lecturing the intention and being insightful enough to separate the successful from those who simply dream.

In order to place a ten-year plan, at the end of the day, our own interests are compatible with mutual aid. Since the opportunity reverses the doubt, we remember the good intention can transform surplus into exchange. Generosity, social recognition and public spirit are mixed and it's worth exploring the debate on reciprocity. I hope we found it a while ago. It should be added, corporate boards influence decisions. This can lead to delays to convincing in high stratospheres. However, it's a matter of leading communication since money is not a problem. Those advocating for expansion in a 30-way wisdom may need details in advance about projected earnings before interest, taxes, depreciation and amortization. At this rate, we will not do it out of respect for inside operators. They already have that marked line, and the beauty is that each club sees it differently, because the methods vary. Why do we wait for a tycoon or consortium interested in establishing an expansion franchise? The sense is attack it from the inside capabilities.

On the contrary, in internal band would be curious enough to discover something new between the influence of the game. The positive disposition of all the interested parties within the organization could be verified. That is, the cost and shared work for future remuneration. That is, the potential of domestic economic power is formidable fiber. Daily operations seem too intense to deviate from reality. Nothing should shake the current course of play. The project would have to demonstrate singular charisma by placing some strengths and a lot of opposition. Scandals have passed and will pass. If your team is five games away from the "Wildcard" and there are twenty days left in the season, will the operations take care of the other business parallel to baseball? No one knew how to convince people with the power of judgment better than the Magnificos. The vital thing on board was the confidence to see the thing since the 2004-year that Andrew Zimbalist published May the Best Team Win, Baseball Economics and Public Policy. The distinguished professor in Economics pleaded for reforms in public policies questioning and expediting the immediate. It was time for the barons of the game to finally do things right. By then, it was the decade in which agreements with great influence would finally be achieved, resulting in today's billions.

Twenty-three years in the future, baseball has multiplied tenfold. There are no strikes by players or referees. The antitrust exemption remains intact. The threats of the owners to move the franchise have diminished almost to zero. With a run of more than two decades without interruption of the game, MLB and the Association of Peloteros already sealed the last collective bargaining agreement (CBA) that ends in 2021.

The executives would never accept such a voluptuous move, until checking if the project contains the persuasive ingredients. We would have to try and explain until comprehension crawled upstairs where Residente had his roundtable. It would be necessary to nurture knowledge and point to the permeated capacity in bad times and in great moments. It would be to continue believing that our favorite pastime follows the great game of extracting and distributing wealth for the satisfaction of many. This was about advancement of product, and we would not veer onto other pastures.

The thing is serious. The corporate foundations along with the infinity of techniques and modalities with the philosophy of inspiration, motivation, and information, are forthcoming initiatives to get the tools going—shall the product advancement becomes a priority. In external focus, we are implying the functions that matter—those weighting the reach of those responsible for the decision template. For sure, you'd want the best analysts to put the idea under additional simulation to iron the wrinkles here unnoticed. There you have a workshop for a while, to continue creating alliances seeing the convergence of influence of the players, the Association as allied entity—the agents and the interested parties disagree in interesting ways they can be part of the specifics contractually. Owners of Majors stadiums and farm stadiums have good access to politicians. Of course, corporate owners have a good record working with regional television stations and the small business chain that hugs every franchise. The rest is history and a new instinct.

11

Extra innings

"The economy is like cosmology. An expanding market, like an expanding universe, has unique laws and a local phenomenon."

~ Jaron Lanier
Who Owns the Future

A kind of fraternity converged in Saigón Chiquita. There I met Hiram Máxime. He does not like to be called by his first name, which is a bit of a problem, but he looked like a coach with no hairs on his tongue. Lastly, I think they sold the data without his approval. The buffoons of the Magníficos nicknamed him Residente and now he shaked the dynamics. "The hidden tool in view to the owners, the total gear. Visualize the impact of the Big 30, the players, the owners of stadiums and farm clubs, MLB Community—in short, the pillars, amongst others that will become alliance."

And it was not too late for Alma to get involved in the idea of achieving competitive balance. Of course, Maravilla 77 in advance, had crunched the strategic data. I imagined the leader, as if a first sergeant in the Army, then heard and echo. The group kept silence.

Alma: If firmness is reached, other sports and non-sports entities would emulate it. Any reasoning depends on the balance and progress of the 4 desires: create interest, win, be cooperative and be part of society. But how do we form alliances to make the leap? Would the influence be his strategic diaspora? What is the record of the pillars of the game? Why Baseball has to own the expansion clubs? Now the scrappy electronic girl was the teacher.

Get in people's minds, the lean leader advised me, with no hairs blocking his tongue. As for the girl sent by DARPA, I didn't dare to question her capabilities. That's why Ruperto used me as an advisor, and the answers to the questions that his expertise did not reply, for that wonder with artificial intelligence could gossip the hell of Magníficos. Don Ruperto remained in tandem until the moment he reclined from the totuma branch, a broad tree. He was a serious expert, and Máxime was for a moment immobile imagining who could be convinced that BAM has won the choice and has the ability to handle expansion franchises. I took notes, and the group didn't question the way they squared the pod. Gradually everything evolved with a view to seeing the thing from the outside.

The important thing is that we all had experience from the outside, I'm an outsider, a loner. No one played professional, including me for being clueless and good people with everyone. The route to improve with enough organization and malice. Who should we convince? The Commissioner and the Executive Board, to those of influence, economists, those with marked interests, the innovator, an analyst, or will it be the one who reveals in the background the magic of symbolism to create private opinion? It could be the Commish's. Maybe convince the one that the game brought her same happiness that we both perceive, because in the end the ball is a matter of playing as a team. We have to celebrate celebrating triumphs. No doubt we are speaking in plural and plurality is the secret of the game, its structure, and the path by which baseball can ensure the flow to the rhythm of the action format. Forward and march. Whether in the field of play or in the "front office", or during weaving for a better future, at the end of the day one has time to submit a report with opinions stepping on the pitching rubber for as long the delivery recognizes professionalism in the matter and to decide the optimal easy play we come to compare and to measure the power of that type of influence. Many of the wishes about the growth of the game have been achieved, not by following a prescribed process but by reacting to the opportunities, since freethinkers think based on individual club design. At the executive level, we could consider the design that captures the modelers of the future once it is known that the resources are upon split to advance the bivouac.

Today, the distribution of profits, whether as a result of luxury fines entering the central fund, the incredible profits from BAM are very good. They fulfill their function of competitive equilibrium. Because of the competitive balance, now nobody threatens to move the franchise. Society is astounded by prosperity as never before. Baseball is still strong; however, society has not seen its most formidable impact. If MLB stopped waiting for a billionaire to want a franchise, and instead, unify the internal resources we would be on the same page using the advantage of controlled reengineering. Guess that we'ved tried to close that confrontation by specifying all the potential, including the alliances of compartments, opening up the classical importance of allowing executives to continue thinking in their own way. Very difficult to convoke the convergence club.

12

It must be about competitive balance

"I hope MLB clinics continue to offer the opportunity to many young people from different countries to receive good instruction from the best sport: Baseball."

~ *Félix Feliz*
Días de Sacrificio, Gloria y Esperanza: A Baseball Scout's memories

We agree in unison, although we can not afford to avoid a bad destiny. The game and the benefits must go on at a higher scale. It's up to the executives and the brains in the field to motor the engines. If the trip does not win your heart, we are fired free to join the independent league.

We greatly appreciate the interest and feedback. Shared imagination was our virtue. As in a ball game, the control systems are much better. The economic, political and social influence in the corporate universe flies through the roof.

It does not matter. Our friends in the Magníficos would serve me as stream stones to jump coordination respecting each and every suggestion. When leaving, I would go straight to the printing press. This would begin the priority of believing in individual skills, team knowing the game skills and embracing the random that transports us to extra tickets to not leave without bringing victory home.

At the start, I had sat at the bar of Jardín Cosita Buena and I snapped an Atlas that came as a coin under the seriousness of the main referee. From there I came walking for the speed of extracting possibility that in the end, surely, it would remain in the perimeter of the utopia. And what about those mentors who emulate the mentality, skills and tools? Questioning if, because they were ideal, they commanded something special about our dream of arriving to the big tent, and together with great social contributions, for example, the tireless sacrifice developing youth sport. Now the way the player is wrapped is unprecedented. Look to see the emphasis on Quisqueya, Curacao, Puerto Rico with the Rubio fever, good talent leaving Cuba and even in Venezuela between lives submerged in constant and deep crisis. The boys of twelve, fourteen years with potential in sight to a prompt contract and the tendency in the formative of players in the academies led by distinguished. The context of the Academy has been an indisputable strength. In 1987, the Los Angeles Dodgers opened Campo las Palmas, the visionary Dominican baseball academy of Ralph Ávila. His many professional signers include Pedro and Ramón Martínez, Raul Mondesí and José Offerman. The historian Alan Klein wrote in his book Sugarball: "Nothing typifies the new direction of Dominican baseball as much as the baseball academy, an institution rooted in the growing presence and benevolent paternalism of American baseball interests in the country." Ralph Ávila built the first baseball academy in the Dominican Republic in 1977. In his description of the baseball academies in the Dominican Republic, Alan Klein wrote: "What the academy does working with Dominican players goes beyond teaching the skills of They teach professional preparation, socialization and how to face the cultural changes they will face in the United States Beautiful concept with the mystery of the day What does society have to not do with Home-Grown? It is obvious, the idea is not new. the action of allowing the youth leagues to continue playing ball to the individual The HomeGrown would be the coordinator in socialization. Shall we implement it to strengthen the Major expansion team? The central current would adopt it, also as an axis and mainstream Baseball will think of establishing in every city to anchor the whole bowl of wax.

With this I returned to reality, and I deduced now the model had potential to be cloned. The point would be to convince the Magnificos to see the figures. On the big screen was Aroldis Chapman in the ninth inning drilling the batting zone and the sound of the ball cutting the air created a feeling of uneasiness. From here on, by continuing to think about a conceptual framework that leads to improving competitiveness and bring wealth while reformulating baseball in the community, the crossroads of making radical changes by chance, consensus, learning and business design can not be underestimated. It would be for these styles of change that we are close to executing the activity beyond thought and strategy to a future reality.

At the end of the day the executives have in their field-book to realize that the adventure is not about changing parts, but to adapt as if it were jumping from an initial system to a new one. The clubs give the same round every day, except that in the baseball you do not have to tie the tie to anybody. The initiative does indicate requirements to make dramatic changes in a relatively short time. We would say that the total system of MLB would undergo structural transformation and some relevant processes that will affect competitiveness, we hope for improvement. It would be to take the measure with the interest of the fanaticada and income potential and continue to do the best that MLB can, while executing at the top of other sports entities. Individual competition now possesses balance in a constant grinding where mental errors cost games. The goal becomes larger by studying the roots of individual success that reflects collective and governance credit. And as an organization, MLB has no problems, but it is possible that it can improve the handling of complications in a fresh challenge. It knows well inside the endless work of the experts. From the beginning of the game there were people with influence for maneuvers outside the league. No other sports entity continues to fly high, holding strong through the most difficult times and bouncing back better than ever. However, how could we avoid careful thought of spinning ideas that could trigger reflective dilemmas?

Speaking of competitive balance, in 2013 the Houston Astros came out of the National League and joined the American West League. Since then, the universe of parity has fifteen clubs in each league. However, the thought of expansion has not disappeared. It may not happen immediately, because as long as it does not materialize it does not prevent you from formulating a parallel scenario. Not putting a head in it can result in another opponent applying the pod, and then the unit of effort would remain foreign to common sense. Forgotten.

The geographic growth is possible if it is assisted of the money derived from the luxury tax and the redistribution of the payroll of the team (first obtain the approval of the association and other ways exist). Before putting it into operation, the distribution of the income will be shown as all the MLB components know how to negotiate the interests. In another pandora's box we could appreciate boxes and circles playing the power tower, with arrows and arcs pushing the sensitive direction buttons, but we will turn the keys in the lock announcing that developing mental simulation is also not 'coconut' (who said it was not easy).

Welcome to the return of the Expos at the Olympic Stadium. Greet the franchise based in the San Antonio Alamodome. Can Utah develop a winning franchise? Oklahoma has oil, in Portland there is a market and good heat in Las Vegas. Too much to ask. Things heat up at the borders of the leagues. Montreal has fought for a return. The chosen regions are the exception in case the unified decision and their own judgment take the game to another table.

Imagine the embeleco adhered to the brand of fresh clubs and in operational support to MLBAM as a control valve, the players, sports agents, owners and sponsors in commitment to investment and total quality of the project. The ball is expensive, but it is sufficiently dynamic achieving the goals to set an example to other entities.

13

It's a challenge alright; not impossible

"If a political party or religious sect had even a fraction of the influence that the advertising industry has on us and our children, we would be on the warpath."

~Rutger Bregman
Utopia for Realists: How We Can Build the Ideal World

The boys quartered in Wonder 77 were moving at a thousand revolutions. They were generating insight into the individual parts of day-to-day practice in all media planning, measuring time, maximizing contacts and technology, managing contracts, negotiation and continuing education. Basically, planning wide is curiosity-I was told-so much so that to know a topic is to try to scale its level to a point where the potential of consultant or consultant is palpable. You also have to do the psychiatrists.

I pulled several books off the shelf. With force, I opened any book and its wonders to understand the transformation. Despite what emerged, the expanding control manual resided inside. The Central Fund is key, or you can have another exclusive fund for expansion. It is not a transparent core, at least for external observers, but the Central Fund is vital to many social programs like MLB Community. Programs for the development of the game, support of precious projects such as RBI, Pitch, Hit & Run, MLB Youth Academy, Boys & Girls Club of America and valuable support in commitment to the fans, the municipality, and effort to remunerate the veteran players for tireless work, and the earthly environment that sets the game. The direction and splice of promoting the game are marked. Taking off from there any squad in celestial belt could begin to weave the internal plan without discarding that neither the intention is not to exhaust the social piggy bank.

Something like not to reinvent the wheel, MLB faces the sacrifice of maintenance, and from the external monitoring we see many storms in there to keep the interest in the game high. In fact, and again assuming that the 2018-2019 period was analyzed in order to penetrate the expansion regions, we first look for the ideal ones. If they are from the Millenialls stock, they all qualify for recognition squad.

Why is not there a national high school ball tournament? Taking the initiative with an aggressive attack with youth leagues, supported by existing community programs, talking with Parks and Recreation. It makes a big difference to break the paradigm that professionally molded talent is still a cone. Many players return to town some share the secrets of the farm and the dressing room. For these ideal, would be to eat a mofongo with caldito, and the impact must be overwhelming. Finally, a coordination so that the local leagues feel the impact of the training, the advice to the chiquillada, ways to block the ball so that they do not score, and the scourge of the marketing hung to the effigy of the players. All the attached qualities, the environments where we played ball, the battles with curves and dizzying lines direct to the handle. By tradition the advance of the game is based on preparation and the security of the experience provides the edge of the attack. What if this were the direction in establishing the brand of expansion franchises?

Of the luxury taxes collected and other sources of income, MLB executes the distribution to teams as part of the agreements with the Peloteros Association and among the owners of equipment. The local distribution, with the modern advances of accounting and transfers are the star topography in any antagonistic with the suggestion of going to plot the global integrity. The first blow to expansion is the sending of the greedy platoon in grinding to wield the benefits of professional experience. There is still to be extracted from those powers that compose and share the total effort, although we are placing an organization with thirty clubs, thirty stadiums, thirty different philosophies and each club subscribed to nine farm teams. And what of the Regional Sports Networks? Many are owners and others-property of the equipment, but there is a lot of creaking on the way to capitalize on the flow with excellent signal wherever you want.

It's said Victor Pellot was born with a first base mascot by hand. He had safe hands, and by purposely dropping the ball for double-killing, the Majors instituted the "Infield-Fly" rule. Through the path of a game, we can formulate recognition, draw from the experience and global objective, and bring expansion to the home, and in turn institute and model the imbalances of the game and its composition. Through the fantastic, without suggesting Tony La Russa, Cheito Oquendo, the inventors of the Hall of Fame, all the executives and operators in the teams know the process and requirements when establishing a franchise. Riding an expansion franchise costs money, it takes human resources with a variety of specialties, players, scouts, leadership and even more important-voice and vote of the entire structure. The best help to the club is to execute at the height of the powerful, intelligent and agile fiber that we know. Making reference to strengths, opportunities, weaknesses and threats is synonymous with spreading the threads of the ball. What does the scorecard say? What does the merchandise report say?

The Players's Association, for example, should never change its role as a labor union. Of course, conditions and concerns will arise, and it is best to placate at the same negotiating table with fervor to the extreme of optimism. In the question of win-win, there is no better example as mutual commitment being responsible for better geographic depth in baseball. Pray for the pitcher's best friend and let the manager not touch his arm in this direction. In simplistic mode and by principles, before verifying major challenges, it would be very important that all parts of baseball continue to function in action and responsibility with flexibility in the face of radical change. I do not believe there is a difficult obstacle to overcome, carving the batting lineup in descending order, looking at the causes of the current state. Markets responding and that fills a mileage, maybe another spider web to advance the game. It doesn't make sense to stay put and wait for Murphy to land his parachute. If the decision template reveals a forward march, start on the foot that leads to growth. Thinking in growth; in how to get it signifies assets in motion. Resources that guarantee victory tend to hone on gaining physical and abstract territory. Money assists in growth, yet other assets require visibility be given equal share. Humans make the difference. We have super computers. Organization and work are easier. Baseball is composed of elements that mastered all facets required to be designated as sport. American baseball is great in her battling theater, the hint of a force to be reckoned with if you've been about to be convinced.

Showing deep appreciation of the value of the gigantic and compact allies in the theater puts us in the seat of balancing evaluation of strengths and weaknesses. This baseball has done superbly so far, and the tendency is to achieve more. Balance competing is not the only major factor—she has resolved to take it up a further step.

14 |
Suspicions work the simple

"This world is about the business of creating champions in conditional societies to worship them and reward the best with compensation over $100 million."

~*Mathew Futterman*
Players: The Story of Sports and Money, and the Visionaries Who Fought to Create a Revolution

It was in the 1950s when the minor leagues expanded. Branch Rickey had a lot to do with it, like almost everything that requires wide vision in baseball. Assuming that television complements the visit of the adversary announcing the power of player development and teamwork end up among the priorities in a children's game played by adults. The experience of the people who run baseball in the field and beyond the dressing rooms take advantage of the invention of training in a series of disciplines. Down in the yard the guideline to the troop to expand the game does not need mental blocks. On the one hand, the game is slow, technology is doing it faster, and it remains the favorite game of so many. In this, opinions vary, the fans sometimes moody because of the high cost. As a constant prelude to who cares is synonymous with free will. Free play, and if the concurrence to the stadium and streaming digitally rises, then the game continues to be popular and producing. In 2017 fourteen clubs brought in between 30,757 and 46,492 spectators on average playing at home. Teena Maddox, veteran writer of the digital magazine TechRepublic produced in the same year that "the technology is being used to accelerate the game experience so that teams can keep fans coming to the stadiums, as well as to buy merchandise, food and beverages. Since 2012, attendance has been slowly decreasing in MLB games, with fewer fans opting to navigate traffic around the stadiums and pay high prices to watch their favorite teams." Also, emphasized in 2007, the busiest year in league history, 79.5 million fans attended regular season games. In 2012, this figure fell to 74.9 million and, in 2017, fell further to 72.7 million, according to Forbes. However, the MLB.TV subscriptions are listed number four after Netflix, Amazon and Hulu. In 2016 the famous sports commentator Maury Brown, said in Forbes, "while digital media continue to see a large part of the revenues of the leagues, television continues to grow and now appears as the main revenue generator."

On the other hand, as amateurs, actors, intellectuals or executives or simply, the modern trends impel us to believe in growth. The latter have lived the necessary regulations to adjust the relationships of individuals with voting rights and empower them for purposes of social exchange and material among equals. Arguing to the achievements and coexistence between players and owners and relationships between all the characters in the clubhouse. Anywhere the business flourishes, there's a sense of unity and focus on precise goals always prevail. Anyone who appreciates the sport or part of it knows that being in favor of a greater good means taking the political entry while the practice precedes the prediction, and the risks involved in such a vertiginous path. The adherence to social virtue in the golden rule is to concentrate on the level of power and current influence, inclusive activities and so organic in the opportunities that this can pick up.

You should never underestimate who is going to allow a formidable opposition. The author from Piedra Candela had spoken.

Why are players and influence agents the correct options to take on the advance of the product? The initial investment (shared resources) serves as a transfer of valuable skills that constitute the maximum exchange of knowledge in the wings of perfection. It is not a lie that the game is prosperous. The owners are billionaires, and they are corporations. Players and agents are millionaires, and arena bosses are adept at manipulating politics and exploiting interest-based fiscal shortcuts, leaning towards the national political climate. Before dissecting the point, the Internal Revenue Service has legal laws. Some are introduced as advantages, but in case of doubt, follow the legality and for the seventh entry, winning can be crystal clear. Take the example in Section 501 (c) (3) of the Internal Revenue Service, which, according to David Cay Johnston, is "such a dark tax law that the IRS has practically ignored, as it authorizes individuals and businesses to deduct gifts made to charities Fixed in subsection 15 authorizes tax exemption for insurance companies As a result of the tax reform law of 1986, the requirement that tax-exempt insurers be mutual companies was imposed, owned by those who bought the policies-investors could now own under the tax-exempt insurance companies." The author of Perfectly Legal adds that by the year 2000 there were more than 1,400 of these companies, today savoring the benefits of investments. Would it be reasonable to paste this resin to the new grind of expansion?

As to the talent available for another level, although it is difficult to find, sign and nurture it, it is no less than the effect of the era of the metric turning in favor of placing resources during the preparation to win games and series. The general managers have made the most of what is available by following talent with a scarcity mask, but reality contains enough. It looks scarce because of the temperate demand in the competition. There is now a lot of depth of resources available among the 30 clubs.

The difference in the panorama of the tables of positions and victories is the application of the prognostic advantages, clarifying that the meaning of thinking about utilities in part of the owners is a summons to the power of decision. Those interested in formulating a launch platform are made to think that the forecast domains have their terrain ready. Based on resources, we would say.

By the time the prognosis greats come together, assign their priorities there will be an environment of possibility, until the trends, the machines, the "sabermetrics" brains, the algorithms, the interested ones and their accountants say go, seen not possible, it would be modified to influence millions of people. The rest is to find out what is needed to not lie on the other side of the train and being left behind in the face of so many tactics and strategy in the lessons cooperating.

If it were only for the domains to formulate a thesis, without assuming suspicions work the simple. The comprehensive, today is solved by the tamers of quantifying machines of baseball physics and the flow of dollars based on a specific doctrine. They have at hand the manual of the subjects that bring prosperity to the sport. See that these wise men reside on the stands and others fan the "Yadi Molina" effect. At the moment, there is demand for the tempered of the competition between teams. There is a lot of good catchers. Although the trends indicate a surplus of forecasts-it remains the contact of the people running the organization the handlebar to not lose balance and project weakness to the antagonist who may come dressed inaction. So, yes, it takes the tulivieja to the bamboo fence.

Does it mean that it is now another story? The models to reach the largest audiences and alliances carry a correct purpose and objectives so that it was built in a lot of face-to-face coordination. Companies that do business in markets must be in tune with government rules. It is a question of detecting the strengths that the region enjoys, therefore, developing enough to take off parallel to the economy. The story may reveal the meaning of circling the Alamodome, not with weapons and horses, but embedded in that the new franchises must survive. The brand of the franchise that springs from the commitment to create prosperity, and nothing prevails unless teamwork is shown. For those who care about the game and its geography, the stronger the majority opinion, San Antonio can proliferate without affecting the markets of the Astros and the Rangers. Those teachers in this charge faithful fans long ago.

Welcome to the product advance. And before going to sleep for being tomorrow the day of carrying breastplate and mask on the banks of the river, time to organize dreams and in dreams there is a fixed structure. One unfit to work reengineering unless you persuade the persuasive in a simulation that requires thought because of its complexity. Let's remember the rest is history, now that the arrival of a hybrid system connects the strengths of the sport with the community. Let's analyze some key domains. Owners, players, the Association of players, those running the machinery of minor leagues, including scouts, umpires, analytics in "Sabermetrics", and of course, general management make up functions, a great complement to the power of executive decision. The points of opinion are relative to the consideration of the executive capacities before the disposition to take the fiber to the end in unified mooring.

15

Sounding like a broken record: the time is right

"You had to go in and out. The zone did not belong to the hitters; it belonged to the pitchers. Today, if you pitch inside, the umpire warns you. I don't think it's fair."

~Juan Marichal, the Dominican Dandy

The world is somehow chaotic, but powerful conglomerates thrive. Every day many new associations, in which someone is in charge and those in the chain of command, prefer the action of the delegates to receive later the routes of advice to connect, how the key elements digest the mission against the restrictions based on the resources allocated. The resources allocated are the powerful use of assets according to their capabilities. Looking for a scheme to present a scenario with such a balance could direct the effort of product advance based on whether the unified strategy is hanging from the Grand Paradigm and how the domains would run the last "dog-n-pony show" on the avenue.

In performance, MLB has traced its sharp corners in the tactical and strategic theater, while the box office depends on how high the stairs are climbed to distribute resources, as no one better does. She who has considered her participation in baseball as an adventure is not a work lover until the attitude shows. Between the glossary of autonomy-commitment and learning-the central operating fund-the new identity in the rivalry category seeks the democratic focus in the head of any analyst.

Who will pay for the expansion? National media stations with astronomical figures in their banks could disburse half of the costs. I refer to the regional sports networks in the breadth of operations parallel to market signals. During the years of strikes by players and referees, there was an emphasis on the fact that team owners had to invest in alliance with television networks and all the means to prepare for astronomical salaries about to explode. The allies in taking the game to the theater at home decided to buy portions of the major franchises. For this business exchange behind the show, we understand the global situation has more security nodes, probably the prominent feature if you want to maintain competitiveness, and if the legal and regulatory prescribes it. During the decade of n

The nineties, there was dynamism in the markets, between the uncertainties of the real estate bubble and the collapse of stock markets. Without alludes penetration in the risks, in economy there is the great force of chance. The impact of economic chance in the current era is the result of recovery.

By strengthening the tactical and strategic faces are seen. Money matters, and things have changed. Planning in partnership must be the heavy effort in the expansion. The owners can own a fiber of fresh bread. How much money do the 750 players earn if the average salary is 4 million? Three billion or in the stadium. The construction of six clip stadiums of $ 400 million makes $ 2.4 billion dollars. The public sector puts financial leverage in the stadiums. The investors are already in the circuit. Baseball has never been so big and profitable mitigating the risks or converting public funds for the construction of the stadium. Now there is an established and precise route to continue functioning in the way that the structure allows minimum adjustments in its parts. Leadership and outstanding results in most ventures deserve joint credit.

While passing over first base anchoring rubber to second, modernity makes us understand its powerful position to change in tune with contemporary advantages. In order to evaluate any strategy, there is an eagerness in the assets at hand or those in the economic yard available. Whenever the mandate is resource intensive, it is true, baseball has two sides: head or tail, game, or business. In the order of the game and the development of the team and winning series, the other side manages the capital and its technical maneuvers. The game's leaders have shaped a unique balance in entertainment and economic gain in a growing era in technological advances and accuracy to dominate the competition. Dictating deep goals remains a challenge, but the circumstance is to share success at a formidable pace, and that is an opportunity for wide thinking in the midst of the battle already almost won.

High and clear and definite that the markets are going high as a better indication, and at least the voice in one of the references suggests that the orthodoxies in the game play their part in the proposal. The decisions of the "playmakers" have a lot to do with the seriousness of maintaining the game in the human domain, of course, with technology in the palm of the hand. It means then that the forecasts attract the antagonistic and the doubt. To force coarse reengineering would be to scratch the traditional characteristics of the Sport and no doubt we would force the invisible man who does not become visible long ago to materialize shortly. It comes to verify the last credential product of the registration card for specific purposes. Despite the sport being so strong and satisfying, in its registry, geography is not a focus on current reality. No great idea goes unnoticed without historical tradition, but the hunt for the phantom of uniformity will not be in sight unless you bring an alliance that foots the bill and fosters interest in the game.

Expansion in this way is one of the many maps to display the success of the MLB Industry Growth Fund (IGF) since its inception in 1997, and now integral to the Collective Bargaining Agreement. The IGF increases the interest of the fans, increases the popularity of baseball and guarantees the growth of the industry. The MLB Competitive Balance Tax finances the IGF. The Players Association and individual clubs provide additional funds.

The models of reaching the greatest alliances with the right purposes and aims already have been built in much face-to-face coordination. Baseball does come to town in strange forms. Nolan Ryan and an also iconic sponsor like H.E.B. San Antonio have model politics; it's inclusive. Corporations doing business in the region are in tune with government rules. It's a matter of sensing the strengths a city enjoys, hence, developed enough to take off along the additional economy ups and downs as many other opportunities will circle the Alamodome. And that goes to all new franchises and those in charge of their establishment, as the branding of the franchise must germinate by hints only prosperity determines. The facts from previous expansions take the back door to the wisdom of executing on gut instinct. Maybe time's going too fast, as three sets of generations run baseball now. They run the world. Plotting and executing complex battles in a geographically assembled theater requires bold imaginaries with the "bottom line approach" to maneuver the organization into actions. It may take you an extra meeting to confide a heads-up warning.

For sake of competitive balance, in 2013 the Houston Astros departed the National League and joined the American League West. Since then, the universe of parity has fifteen clubs in each league. Nevertheless, the thought of expansion has not gone away. It may not happen any time soon, for while it won't materialize, the glory among similar professional entities most brainstorming on I advances in meeting unity of effort.

Every spinning idea is nothing more than additional brainstorming capitalizing on current success to strengthen equitable balance for all, including the fans sitting in and order ketchup over fries. Therefore, there goes the first hit on a liner over second base on the tickets war. Geographical growth is possible assisted with the money derived from the luxury tax and redistributing team payroll. At the end of the line, revenues distribution will show as both sides know how to negotiate interests. I envision better salary during the restriction and free agency periods. In a springboard, we could appreciate the boxes and circles, the arrows pushing onto direction.

Nevertheless, telling a baseball story in this fashion seeks to tap into the organizational structure. Check it out, shake it and assign it a figure in potential. Alike, a good baseball story still sounds like an exciting brain-storming talk in the spooky candle-lit patio in every child. In my case, it was long ago. The electricity poles hadn't yet arrived by helicopter—a prognosis of a tale, my grandmother said: "The game will grow; it will trust each of its great industries, positioning players in the central role in capitalism operations. The game will move to many cities and countries."

I didn't catch a lick, so I made it part of the narrative on the back of the Topps baseball cards. I was about nine years old holding a hand-carved guava tree bat, heavy as a Caterpillar road-flattening machine. I learned to read and write before five because Mama and my aunt didn't. They bought on credit in the market on the top of the "barrio." Many times, payment was delayed. Unhappy faces. But people in my town supported one another. The conversation faded into time. The candle went off. How would I benefit almost sixty years from that scrounge cellophane note? Still a geographic reference in the back-and-forth brushes of time. It may be baseball's disposition isn't geographical or that my grandmother was in reflexive counsel that no matter wealth, the pleasure is developing action in a scenario that imbues an elementary procedure disassembling the present moment, separating known, unclear and the presumed to decide wise.

Beyond imagination, it doesn't take additional conscience to realize the sure way baseball can get bigger and better. And there's no exact way to write it in a story. No precise on how to include the academy concept as part of the farm subscriptions. Assume everyone wants decent contenders, increase in revenues, willing to get away from building the new stadium fairy tale, brainstorm on considering the cost fans shell to support the game we love, and hear no more "we're moving our franchise." Feel free to scan the vicinity to gather how hard is getting to win the World Series, but that's been the traditional reality as the sport grew. No past expansion outfit experienced the advantage of forged partnership and collective support from various angles. Newcomers indirectly will increase unified value to all participators. The support we can build developing local baseball cloning the Urban Academy and RBI could be the jewel that gives you tax breaks without resorting to loopholes, being the function of Baseball's leadership in charge of oversight. The initial investment (shared resources) serves as a transfer of valuable skills that constitute the ultimate sharing of knowledge on wings of perfection.

To the fan of big events, statutes and other organizational pieces with moving parts tend to shape decision-making abilities. It's like logic placement, models of cause and effect, effective guesswork, different facts and different interests and the thirty other ways to cook a C-Rations can of peanut butter. In other themes, a good choice is similar to having a nice wide screen, the Yankees, being able to drop the cards face-down with the statistics up to be analyzed. On a time- scale, ten years seems too short. Search discovery in all the good in the international reach and you've met the source of future wealth. The soil has been seeded.

Municipality

Who said the communities with expansion potential got a voice? We could number variety of instances about approaching challenges smartly. That said and concentrating solely on field competition, putting a winning squad together the Consortium for Montreal ought to determine the Expos brand is just dormant due to previous existence in the big grind. The future of organization focuses on "wants" over the old method of needs. The Expos, knowing the ground the big markets hold, may want to emulate the fastest path to championship like the Kansas City Royals just a few years back. Montreal is the largest city in north America with no Baseball club, and if the challenge is the stadium, there ought to be alternatives to bypass whatever is keeping the region from Baseball's prosperity.

Machiavelli might have had a better example. It has to do with acquiring depth. The Royals done it, other traditional powerhouses failed to perform at the level, likely due to known reasons. Similarly, the Cubs, Astros and Pirates have adapted their future to clubs liable to do extremely well soon. Look at the rays, how marvelous. Look at Pittsburgh and Chicago as sure National League wildcards in recent years until Cubs went bizarre in 2016. Like with the chokehold on Billy the Goat, the Cardinals, in 2015, bathed in tradition and team-building expertise clinched a postseason berth ahead of all. The story of St

Louis dates from time before time, and somewhere down history, suggests the greatest adapts to changes faster. Past having to decide the kinks in a long season that starts when the hawk is chilled and ends snowing, the Blue Fabric Group shouldn't have any problems in shifting gears. League realignment is relatively easy and interesting. Still to decide whether interleague play will continue, as the trends indicate it's good for the game. For the first time, Baseball would be rightly distributed geographically—not merely the tip of the lance in the proposal. But whether we begin on mapping components of this sport we call "pastime," be it necessary to make baseball decide its destiny.

16

It isn't like eating a prohibited mango across the fence

*"Even though you only have three strikes, you're still not out.
There's always something you can do. "*

~Tony La Russa
One Last Strike

The latex gloves we wore in the backpacks, given on the third floor of the Ernesto J. Castillero Library, were witnesses for hours browsing the old and cracked leaves of the Panama Star & Herald. One rainy afternoon I found out that the library has a copy of Panamanian Baseball History. I got into the Ford truck, went to Parque Omar, talked for a while with Mister César at the desk about Weaving Baseball. Nearby, Rupert, in gloves, was hoarding the Herald at the back table. I noticed that Mr. Irregular felt on a piece of paper the names of descriptive and colorful teams like Aspinwall Baseball Club, The 20th Century, Columbus Baseball Club, The Stars of the Pacific, Panama Athletic Club and The Emerald of the Isthmus. I knew then the old man was plotting to weave something on the roots of the isthmian ball. That's why I looked for the 'gallero.' The man who told fables to the children of the mountains between Boquete and Volcán had an extreme. He did not give a damn about the rules. He did not worry about conventions, obligations, or completing the return when following regulations and protocol. We noticed he was quite nonconformist, guided by the opportune thing. Being outlawed was his gift for advancing his own interests, and this did not mean additional work for the right index finger, but Ruperto was also flexible and the intellectuals at the annual Book Fair at the Atlapa Convention Center considered him an expert. Some countrymen regarded him as dissident, and itt didn't matter. We had another challenge—the social climate in Continental U.S. it's frightening. Proliferation of drugs, weapons, gangs, polarization between races, sudden motivation for laziness against physical activity, and never missing the clandestine plane.

In expansion, the HomeGrown brings the proximity of active and retired players. It would be an interesting clash among those interested in each recreational table in the municipality; between the visibility of the competition; and between some economic wheel that can leave the great axis under partial reform. The creation of the HomeGrown academy, not only the Dominican image, but the expansiveness of coordinating the community youth leagues, because we must be willing to change suddenly and catch any support from the public as if the voice and vote of the fanatic sealing the agreement.

The value of the elements would dictate being the primary potential for unified success. As we were loosening the threads of the fabric, we thought of control, of taming the beast of inconveniences. For that negotiation and resolution of conflicts. Since these illustrious dominate what can derail the flows to the bank, we do not need to use external consultants if among the operators you can select the successful experiences of production, and that is what is ironed out. Common sense has knocked on the door a while ago. The evidence in store in all the clubs much reinforces the forecast.

Maybe it's the seventh sense, or when a series of offerings is presented for you to choose the best tools is to hammer the way. In the dynamics of contemporary competitivity the particularities on both sides of playing and producing money dictate a lot about the next move and that essence must be seen from the outside. How those with more intimate friction see it-the media and shoe sellers-and how hard it is to convince the professional inside. Clinging to the minimum in every positive aspect, but the reform formula goes further so as not to underestimate a system that has fought here and there. The project loads fabric for an ironmonger. All the time we have been organizing how to climb the hill. It is a new era in sports. Teacher Rick Horrow said it. For 2011, the fans were the designated drivers of a $750 million business. Since then, the digital era and its endless menu of options, from the coverage of the game to the proliferation of fantasy games that simulate reality. The scenarios help us to think in years ahead, how the game in product now becomes easy to understand and understand. What if we could place capitalist power and shortcuts in the tax code? In its absolutest it presents a force in the position of figuring the meaning to the incognito. For then it is a matter of entering to question how you can download a badly calculated hype for a bullfight.

Super! This is not coconut shell. Then we define the characteristics of domain analysis remembering that the archetypal fiber (of the behavior based on its attributes) of baseball focuses on the development of that activity that attracts us, is smart and shrewd in a school game that does not occur either. nothing. If it were not for the analysis as the story transforms, there would be no deep vision of a better tomorrow based on the results obtained. How successful is organized baseball? Is there a secret in the function method? Something of extreme impact to this conversation? Oiver the blonde of Piedra Candela, and pupil of Ruperto was familiar with the game on the shelves of the Ernesto J. Castillero Library. He moved to the city on behalf of the Americans, something related to the girls in the call center in Quarry Heights. Wine with experience carved north of Boquete, the beautiful and fresh village on the banks of Río Caldera. He turned on the monitor thinking how to eat a mango on the other side of the fence:

"Tell me Alma, and if the change in the Rule 5 Draft had not been so crucial."

"Yes Analytic. Confers the same coincidence: yesterday you woke up and asked if R5D was the panic cure to the expansion draft. I suspect that you suggest all the teams give their prospects and heroes as Hack Wilson, Roberto Clemente and Odubell Herrera; all on the historic shelf of the namesake R5D. I see where the line goes and being able to draw talent with all the draws was crucial. Do you remember the year that the Tigers chose Víctor José Reyes, Venezuelan and teacher of the three gardens? Chosen # 1, almost spent his time to enter the Grand Circuit and with little power at bat. Six seasons in the minors, but suddenly some scout noticed certain tools in the boy from Barcelona, Venezuela. In addition to covering land, he owned .298 at bat and .347 reaching the white covers with straps and a "ground" rod. Not surprising to the exact date in the Sabermetrics, Victor Jose stole 30 bases with the Jackson Generals and the Salt River Rafters."

"I am more interested in the reason of the narrative of expansion and negotiate outside the market if you can merit it internally. I know you're going to oppose, because expansion to 36 occurred every two years, and there are no signs we can reach 40 by 2030. I'm interested in your digital opinion if doubling the 16 entries to Playoffs was good move. Who knows. For the wool when playing intensity of 130 in performance, does not prevent you lose three or four

good prospects. Why not protect them from the R5D? Put on a digital helmet, let's see."

"No amigo, consider it. # 1: There is extra wool, and the dubbing of the playoffs improves the funds available to compete. Those awakened by the expensive luxury tax now have a springboard when paying the fine. The clubs receiving aid according to the rules of distribution take more chance to the postseason with the best 16. # 2: Thank you for converting R5D to a source of talent not put on the roster of 40 to fill ranks in the expansion franchises. That same year Victor made # 1Pick, there were 61 players on the list, primarily pitchers. In simple mathematics, 60 players are a leap to the moans of risking talent for expansion. #3: Something similar had already been done with the draft of the competitive balance since 2017. All the teams in the last ten places in revenue or in the fund among the last ten in market size obtained a selection in Round A, after the first round, or Round B, following the second round. Using a formula that considers the income and the percentage of victories."

"But there are enough players?"

"Only exposing that the R5D power the nervousness by the expansion draft, but it is also remediation."

Right there and then we notice the laundry list of dilemmas, but it wasn't up to us. It was all about friendship and a great bullpen. Calling for an executive meeting be more reasonable. By the bleachers we'd talk on the serious debate of adding dynamics to the postseason.

So much pod for a reformatory meeting, Ruperto babbled. To the other spectrum of qualities, the famous writer of Piedra Candela and his nebulous missions motivated in me the interest to play ball at another level. Before the intense narratives of the master of the highlands now in research on Isthmian equipment named Spur Cola

Refreshers, Old Letter Liquors and Chesterfield Smoker I knew the fabric should consider the opinions from baseball people. Organize by questioning what makes the game great and traditional despite its unknowns and intricacies undermined by modernity.

17 |
Playoffs dilemma

"The ability to gather people in baseball is one of the virtues of honor in our National Pastime. The game allows us an unlimited number of opportunities to create memories for fans and impact the important causes for them. For Major League Baseball and its 30 clubs, this unique stature represents a real privilege, one we honor. "

~Robert D. Manfred, Jr.
Commissioner of Baseball

D uring the playoffs happen cases and things. Stadium workers, contractors, and the media contribute greatly to spreading wealth and popularity. Do you remember the final tables of the 2014 season? The Cardinals won 104 games. The Pirates 96. It was when the Giants with 88 wins eliminated Pittsburgh in the National League Joker. We did not see it as a fair game to the benefits that 96 victories must confer. A series of five games is more interesting and more profitable to the income distribution chain. What do we try to influence? The fruit of a dilemma, the most productive. The fall period is when the contest becomes as profitable as in gladiatorial arena, like in the Wildcard game.

In reality, the Wildcard cheats cities from vital postseason earnings. Whatever statistics may surface from the actual playoffs sc heme tournament of wins and losses is an emotional challenge until the twenty-seventh man falls. In between, media streams our egos with additional lessons shrouded in dilemmas.

On about how you can dump an entire season effort in one wildcard game sounds like nothing out of the ordinary from a truckload of pleasant sizzling summer memories. The wildcard system is a major imbalance. It is true baseball has changed, has potential to remain changing, and its stability means full benefits remain untapped. The wheels of change are always in motion despite the idea this grand old game is unshakable. Perhaps, those in power within the baseball circle may swear the game is still incontestable. While the address goes to Baseball's establishment, let us get concrete on a few spinning ideas deducing organization and play contest are far from its ultimate evolution. Baseball in itself is a prisoner's dilemma. From review of the ground rules to the last out, it's still a game that without a specific strategy, it's either champagne or no cigar. Straight to the options of jumping the fence and staying put on the way baseball is—rather on hidden benefits one of the world's most powerful competitive spirit ought to discover we are not alone in the universe. We live in freedom, in a capitalistic society—we can risk getting our heads fried running through defensive football lines, and we can attempt to score a goal with our heads because one thing: freedom. And that's a motivator as we pursue difficult enterprises. One is never alone at the mercy of an umpire who can't see the outside corner. Unity is the other machine to crank the idea. The idea is that a best three out of five series produce more benefits. The whirling ideas are mine—points to follow in a thoughtful, stern approach to look at the consistency to check the ghost of assumed uniformity baseball has made us believe for as long as we keep filling the park. For as long as we remain glued-on much flashing technological tools, the game wants our faith into the belief of the ages. There is no doubt Old Glory pulls magic in our impression with continuity of tradition richness. With its ability to fancy up genuine colors to cheer on, marketing the big stars and the search for the next 1927 Yankees persist, and the clock ticks away. Along heritage of a game in nine innings, engraved powerful ideas amidst blisters and broken dreams suffice as the single most cherished remnants from those who built the game time before our time. The sensible thing is to convert the wildcards to playoffs and allow better chance of World Series contention, and systematically bring more money to cities. On November 2, 2012, Wendy Thurm wrote in FanGraph: "Using the San Francisco Giants as an example, here's how I calculated the amount of postseason ticket revenues raised in two games in the Division Series:

Commissioner's Office	$28,353,800
Players' Pool	$81,405,020
Texas Rangers	$405,150
Oakland A's	$2,631,955
Baltimore Orioles	$7,180,567
New York Yankees	$10,056,589
Detroit Tigers	$10,331,914
Atlanta Braves	$593,613
Washington Nationals	$5,514,968
Cincinnati Reds	$4,441,532
St. Louis Cardinals	$17,747,976
San Francisco Giants	$20,499,714

Fifteen percent of paid attendance receipts for each playoff game are sent to the Commissioner's Office. Fifty percent of paid attendance receipts from Wild Card games are contributed to the Players Pool. Sixty percent of paid attendance receipts for the first three games of each Division Series are contributed to the Players Pool, and sixty percent of paid attendance receipts for the first four games of each Championship Series and the World Series are contributed to the Player Pool. All attendance receipts paid or not paid to the Commissioner's Office or contributed to the Players Group are shared equally between the two teams of each Series game or the Wildcard game. "

Thurm shows that television revenues go to MLB and are distributed to teams in proportional installments, therefore baseball's profits are prolific on many levels. Doubling those close to the postseason would bring enough wool to many strata. Reaching the playoffs means increasing the club's value. The high prestige of a franchise indicates greater participation in the broadcasting networks, being inclusive of the business, building alliances, and even global reach matters for the multiple routes of economic profitability.

Now we are heading to first base. From start, we perceive the need to verify which cities have the potential for new clubs. We think of the stadiums, the playing roster, the front office. Will the fans come to the park? What will be the strategy to follow the central objective of competing in the field and in the bank? What will be the ideal policy to admit balance and opportunity to reach the postseason? Let's enter the dungeon of knowledge and sacrifice in a simulation with the guts on high. On the back of that that impregnates vigor in the preparation and action as a product according to the conditions, let us not lose focus of how the rest is doing to show so much prosperity. If it is organized as such, it is a persuasive attempt, which implores to test the theory in credibility attire with great attention to risks mitigation and continuity of competitiveness in fair grounds. Too much cutting the corner of the hitting zone. We have been thrown to the lions. Definitively may be an effort in futility, but rich in formidable inconveniences before taming what seems an absurd utopian scribble to the blue auditorium. Indigo color auditorium. That's why the chance of the fortuitous scenario is never lacking. The simulation, and if you do not share it, alive and kicking we are here. Only returns to believe this must conclude a subtle message, if the memory is clouded, because more than germinal to complete product intuits that virtue emerges with humble and simple contribution. This is a unified work by contribution of many sides, some with corners to be polished, never perfect. Here it was not debated, it was carved open the game predicting better visibility of the contribution of clubs and players to the community, for example. It includes an infinity of scenery, for making us the introduction of the always utopian scheme, unless the refined plan comes from within.

Nor were we going to underestimate the crossroads of making radical changes by chance, consensus, learning and business design. Really, does this apply to baseball among its sovereignty? Doubt does not prevent you from simulating at least the agenda and its style. It can trigger the unified decision (the one we do not expect because of how brutal it seems). We would say that the total system of MLB would not suffer changes, but transformation of structure and some processes relevant to the increase of competitiveness. It would be to take the measure with the interest of the fanatic exploiting the income potential and continue to do the best that MLB knows how to do. No scratches, superior to other sports entities.

Ethical to formalities with no shackles. Already these proven facts are used to their maximum efficiency. For prior reliability, the entity will make its independent sense as to the size of the new goal. Making sense of one-self in expansion can transform the distorted from not having accurate information to look through the ideas of advancing baseball as it dresses and how the intrigue will make delivery with creative initiative. Hopefully it forces us to formulate our own sense and decide, because the time is hovering upon us like panhandle sound against skull for not acting timely.

Obviously, to represent compelling impact, we had to match the idea with the facts, before marriage in calculated words. Returning to the origin of the idea knowing that the tool of convincing in the coming years pays attention to the evolutionary path as a total entity, in repetitive, seeing the real path as science, art and skill before a broad but replicable challenge. Manageable? Standing before the screen of positivism, and then to see.

Put rubber and nails inside the three-foot line to first base, with no hidden advantages, since the future does not take prisoners. For a second, what makes Baseball the main candidate to carry out the modification of its structure. It is not necessary to explain everything, but it is a definite and profound challenge, and it gives you something to think about.

The ten-year agenda had an unexpected reengineering picture. We did not know anything about "soccer", but sixteen clubs making playoffs would definitely cause enough profits for the franchises, the players and anybody in the food chain; or simply assume we can assign a figure as a cushion for the expansion sheet balance. There is a wing flying low and with power, distance and frequency very responsible for the current bonanza. MLB Community takes care of everything that permeates the altruistic vision. MLB Community contains your credit and distribution of social support in formidable panorama. It does not seem to be a "quiz" about space, time and decisive, but preparation in logic. Point to capitalize on the positive and channels without hallway or excuses. Then, expansion improves competitiveness and brings wealth while cementing baseball in the community-for the fans and those with a broad perspective to start business should be the initiative to see if we feel the positive rebound. You tell me. What guarantees the Designated Hitter will never disappear? Will it become uniform in the inheritance by which the American League embraced the idea of wrapping high average on base, or adhered to the traditional of high "slugging," or the modern formula of OPS (average on base + slugging) or using the depth of the bench. Emerged and Edgar Martinez, with the Seattle Mariners and produced the clear offense in the type of batting offered by the DH. Edgar always honored his position in the lineup. Batter in 18 campaigns, a damaging quality to enter bases illustrated in average of .415. Observing the board of the blonde of Dorado High School, Edgar sounded the spheroid and nothing more than over his 309 homers, he scored 514 doubles. He brought 1,261 runs to the plate, at bat difficult to get him out. Daredevil giving firewood for extra-bases. Since then, the American League awards the trophy to the best DH in the name of Edgar. The National League could pay tribute to another career pusher. It would be 2019 the campaign in which we interspersed the unpublished use of the Designated Hitter, for simulation purposes, that the waves are tightening. From here we do not know if all this nugget of tamarind is necessary or if it is sweet to savor a super rich baseball with a lot of positive change ahead, now that Edgar will be enshrined in the Baseball Hall of Fame. By perceiving the role of the specialized also carries weight on whether it will take or slow down until the next decade, no matter who carries the carbine in the story—we all need to simulate a battlefield to open opportunities. Baseball has done it fully in the full spectrum and its paradigm of four edges. That is why we would try to continue looking for consistency in accordance with the objectives of the project. If we rampant to penetrate the irrelevant, allow pause, or a deep breath to see if there is a chance to provide the ultimate instinct to an enhanced Baseball. Neither conferring with the spies abroad, nor with the girl of scrap quantum and perequera, no crossroads requires a solution to place the simple, the easy of common sense, the truth of the data, and compare the success to the evolutionary occurrences. Is there the Yadier Molina Effect? The incredible man was free of anyone. Surely the Yadi Effect will connect to the great project that does not resist to maintain static. Giving us the luxury in catching, as pitching coach, and as manager. Hail Mary, it had to be part of the Cardinal Rule. On this basis, we can flaunt common sense. That is, pursuing deep challenges complement each situation in the science of the game. The secret of winning is to manipulate such science capitalizing on what goes on in exemplary axes.

According to Warren Berger, in A More Beautiful Question, what would you do if you knew that you were not going to fail? In other words, take initiative with more confidence. You and I would take some action. Assuming not to remain static and maintain power, the future requires a simulation boot and modeling a knot above, exploiting and permeating every facet of performance. Question: How do the heroes do it? Is there a marked difference? First, everything is questioned. Any quick remodeling must travel in multiple paths. You must delegate the duties of assembling the whole apparatus in business format. Although it is in a facet like this. Imagination. But the Institution continues to expand the product in diverse and adaptable ways, at least in the curiosity of redesigning the current doctrine. To try to jump to expansion would be to see how the industry tempers arbitrary coherence by taking purchases and launches towards opportunities. No giant sports competitor dares to negotiate and cross the stores at the same intensity. Tere is always a claim for a better method, and always imagination touches a mix of determination through experience. From start, he feels that if the last stanza is the chance to advance baseball with such an ambitious pretension, he inadvertently turns to the fusion of moral and political philosophy with analytical tools to judge the culture of sport. Here we are not going to inculcate social cohesion, but the total scaffolding depends on external and internal judgment. Alluding to moral philosophy, weaving baseball, it is planning under the tutelage of experience in the matter of construction, disbanding and transfer of implications. Implications are usually conquerable, despite their conflicting nature. The matter must inform that reaching 40 franchises in one or two decades requires taking advantage of market signals.

18 |
Elegance to cement the horizon

"The typical stadium project costs around 40 percent more than the 'official' figures thanks to costs not reported as free land, shortcuts in property taxes, and public operations and maintenance costs."

~Neil Demause
Are New Stadiums a Good Deal? Baseball Prospectus

An absolute wonder—baseball taught me no matter where you're raised, rich or poor, you still have the chance to humbly drop a branch from a guava tree and carve good improving habits. From the origin of happiness, associating the game composition and trajectory by its impact on intellectual gathering, passion becomes deeper and articulable. Heavier than expected, I held on to mine in a pendulum inspired by the always-young heroes of the fifties and sixties hinging long weight swinging over and near the plate. For hours, often under watchful eye of a frail grandmother who didn't know her age, I perfected the hitter's habit. In a perfect world, most of the time with no shirt and no shoes, I aimed rocks for the old abandoned tin house 300 feet away. I named my bat Guayabo. It was the tool to mimic performance from the true heavyweights. The years caught up with my first World Series in television. In 1968 Bob Gibson picked a 17-strikeout shutout against the Detroit Tigers. By the eras of the Big Red Machine, Earl Weaver's Orioles, and Roberto Clemente's superb functions in the Pirates hood my swing had emulated the whole manufacture. Around this process, grandma encoded her own dramatic version of how Joshua Gibson put a rope in the ocean over the right-center wall of the Sixto Escobar Stadium in San Juan. (Decades back she affirmed.) She had heard a game over the radio in which Satchel Paige had a perfect game going opening the eighth. On the first pitch, the leadoff batter swung a liner in center field, and Satchel ordered the defense to sit down. He struck out the side for a shutout of Santurce and the powerful lineup that included cleanup hitter, Joshua Gibson. Pondering on the essence, little in my intuition referred to the part of the sport as a business, something to be discovered back in the future.

We were naïve. Immersed every minute in the stage where a passion takes off and you remove the glove from the handlebar, sometimes afraid the game takes too much time from the rather wide intellect youngsters must strive. Luckily then, baseball offered a range of educational systems, each, at a wonderful life stage. It became a truly exceptional passion. Baseball worked the notion of don't study algebra for tomorrow if you'll have your Topps cards today.

For you over these pages, don't follow my process. I spent too much time in the river, at knee-level on water running from the pitcher's mound in shorts and the boys hitting a rubber ball upstream. Math homework was rarely done, yet my 5th grade teacher had me (in the math class) explain the meaning and my endowed analytics on seasons and individual career performances. Like when Reggie Jackson found out in Winter Ball, he needed glasses to hit. I designed a dynamite school project with a newspaper cut of Reggie Jackson looking at the moon. He was striking out with the bat wrapped all over, no less he hit 27 homers that winter season, breaking Nate Colbert's record of 26, or ballpark figures.

As to less rambling and more essence, I grew up in a family of four bathed in humility, discipline and curiosity. The jokes had to be baseball related. My older brother was too competitive to my skills. My older sister, too smart, at age nine she emigrated to "outside there," in the eerie talk of my Puerto Rican barrio every time the topic veers on the townspeople that departed in hope of a prosper frontier. Lest mention our grandmother, Cruz, flanked by Aunt Paula (supposedly both couldn't read and write) seem to have acquired game analytics. They cooked well, could tell you the time by just looking at the sunshade on a straight line weaved by the contour of the sand on the patio and the roof of the poorly built wooden house. They storied my ass on baseball tradition—much of the information via messenger of the Majors—Puerto Rico Winter League. Played there since the Spanish-American War, from four to six clubs, the league was always loaded with stars that couldn't play in the Majors due to skin color. It was 1902 when baseball became a pastime, and Grandma; with no record of her birthday kept on reminding us time offers much needed data. She was six when the San Ciriaco storm of 1899 ripped through the island and almost cut República Dominicana in half. Much of a systematic connection of the environment, call it sociology or psychology or grind—weirdly and gracefully attributed to the ever and constant baseball talk has opened my mind, and I hope yours. Understanding the Fabric of Baseball is the key to the package in the challenge. I confess during the course of its design, it's an unsteady bridge which made me think otherwise to cross. Not until retreating and returning as guided by the unorthodox. Through its unweaving, I remained poor financially and rich in economics thinking. To keep it simple and go about the business, we made it, and got experience in analytics way after a program of mentorship and lots of batting practice. The business element depends on performance at the play spectrum. Systematically, my bony skeleton adapted, growing strength and fluidity. Practice makes perfection, and in the process, you think what to make with results. Meanwhile Mama swung in the hammock hoping to keep me there, because had I taken off to play at the riverside sand field, exchange of communications could get hairy. She couldn't get a hold of me for a long while. Many a day she sent out the "discipliner" Auntie Paula to see if indeed I had passion for baseball. In spite, I always came home on my bike named Camella (female camel) guided by darkness or hunger or shall Aunt Paula had whipped my skinny wheels that had a look like Vic Davalillo's.

And there the cycle repeated. In the morning, I dreaded school, had to go. In first grade, she gave me one cent. By third grade I was getting three if lucky to swindle a nickel for a candy named limbe-coco. What incentivized granny to make me feel at levels of consumption value? Simple, all the kids in school needed psychological benefits. Being able to buy a block of coconut candy—or a Mary-Jane lifted and ego, as associating the purpose of the grumpiness of the store owner fitted in the category of analytics. Finding one in exclusive fraternity of "fantasy-collector" goes beyond understanding the business side of that that flows cutting the winds of landing the big one through Mister Polo's window. But luckily if I wasn't feeling the exit velocity of objects flying off the guava bat, hooking the glove on the bike handlebar relieved the strain of not caring about the purpose of algebra. Cotorra (parrot) was the glove grandma weaved for my fifth birthday as game present. I named it and during school recess I loved to show around the five tools of perseverance. Still remember being poor, but rich in the tools that carved great habits, capable of looking back and sifting the important feeling of rocks cutting air in distinct spinning motions while adapting to the weight you carry. Camella carried her own weight in another spinning world that took me down the dirt hills to the riverside sand. That was no different than arriving to a state in which one forms judgment on baseball structure, and the game seems product of unconscious motivation or as an external instance not easy to control—sometimes the focus on how nimble your tools and process that meets the contingency in a simple game. It all falls on the discipline of harnessing the specifics of controlling conditions to complete the play. Thinking about baseball's potential has taught me that suggesting the identification of the gravest concerns transcends the historical record. We must test presumptions under the surface, but consider these concerns differ from person to person, from institution to institution. It all is never crystal, unless we've discovered the truth that upon the ball reaching the glove you don't have a problem—you have a challenge.

Epilogue |

"It is change, continuous change, inevitable change, that is the dominant factor in today's society. No sensible decision can be made any longer without taking into account not only the world as it is, but the world as it will be."

~Isaac Asimov

Thinking in time allows the application of a simulation harnessing every element in this diatribe. David Quentin Voigt, in American Baseball, marked the 1950 timeline as parallel to watching sports on television and acknowledging baseball had become the National Pastime. Meanwhile, making belief it was a Saturday morning payday morning in a Chicago factory, while the foreman's smile handing the check to the workers was the tailor with cloth to cut, the unionist became visible. Negotiating with the Association may have been Baseball's best move to bring benefits from timely forward initiatives ending in the praiseworthy nature of current wealth levels and contribution to a highly deserved wear of the crown of sports. The most profitable sports entity and her prosperity have weaved the elements of the game—each contributing its 130% to teamwork, and it all has to do with unity and unification of resources. The sharing agreement and luxury taxes have paid off.

The comparative puts some energy, an entrenched process and practices navigating the environment in order to align an ideology. That's it in any plan that seeks to bypass the outlier of risk. Managing change in those deep processes and practices, by coincidence, is difficult in larger and older companies. When past Commissioner, Bud Selig favored the idea be brought home for bold persons to grind an attitude and go for a geographic alignment, he was coming from the same vision. He envisioned an arrangement by expansion having sixteen teams in each league. The traditionalists and the modern thinkers clashed on myriad facts and the impossible. Howls were loud, as in baseball one disclaimer moves the next in the exercise of revising how pluses outweigh the minuses. Later we might muse on it if advantageous to your conditioning into the essence of hovering between history and tradition and your take on it counts with your tools at the vest.

Asume it the image of a clear day at the park with few complaints from the fans. With the advent of technology there is a glimpse towards the role of sports. In 1951, a white journalist asked Willie Mays if he had come to the New York Giants to remake the magnificent work of Jackie Robinson, as Robinson had wonderfully broken the color barrier in 1947. Willie replied that manager Burt Shotton told him to go out to centerfield and catch every ball at his reach. It was the declaration of the moment, adding, if you are a black person from Alabama and you want to survive in the white world, you keep your mouth shut, keep your head down, smile at the bad fortune of discrimination and make yourself known as charismatic and through your tools.

It didn't behold Willie Mays is probably the top 5-tools player in the game. His father Willie "Cat" Mays Jr. played in the Negro League, and his mother Annie Satterwhite was gifted in track and field and basketball in high school. At age 16, Willie Mays debuted as regular with the Birminham Black Barons.

Say Hey, it was hard but simple with the tools at your disposition, and ever since it was all about the local citizens evaluating the show, obviously as prowlers to influence Baseball to move forward in international membership promoting a good game supporting the heroes and gaining from the Professionals who earned the right to be part of the game's footprint. Somewhere in the boundaries of eras, varieties of competitive strategies flourished by adding business chains to the boy's game that adults think we can play it better.

Back to moment of restructure with no return, there are ways to denote force changes depend on risk mitigation. Experiencing both constant risk and change, the game perimeter has been mined in prevention and conditioning towards the unexpected. If for any reason it results in bad strategy or bad disposition, at the opposite spectrum feeling indisposed does not mean the den of wolves lurking by the perimeter don't think of your magnet that keeps them in the prowl. It's a thing of employing your assets as the fans expect.

Meanwhile, players hoped to create secret and not-so-secret societies to protect themselves from being bought, sold, reserved, borrowed or kept at low wages. The founders of baseball clubs introduced a lot of magic in the GE-type blender labeled in utilities for entertainment. Playing baseball, then as always, seemed easy, but behind a big catch, a steal of home plate or following a short-hop pick-up to end the inning, confidence sat in playing tools forged on athleticism and content of character. Scouting wasn't easy as now, if you know mathematics and might as well unchain Baseball's power in its explosive capacity.

Marvelous. Why Mike Trout has been associated with the highest WAR? Wins Above Replacement (WAR) is an attempt by the sabermetric baseball community to summarize a player's total contributions to their team in one statistic. The Sabermetrics Fangraph Library says, "you should always use more than one metric at a time when evaluating players, but WAR is all-inclusive and provides a useful reference point for comparing players." That's in case ordinary play and operations remain unscathed, and there's no reason to believe otherwise, note part of play and operations follow metrics to invest and spend a specific amount of money for each victory in both sides of the spectrum. I'm glad I don't know math.

The game is way more intrinsic, go ask the arbitrators.

Who said it will be a walk in the park?

A Curious Mind, by Brian Grazer

American Baseball, by David Quentin Voigt

Bad Sports, by Dave Zirin

!Béisbol! Pioneros y Leyendas Del Béisbol Latino, por Jonah Winter

Baseball by the Numbers, by Baseball Prospectus Team

Baseball's Game Changers, by George Castle

Baseball/Literature/Culture, by Peter Carino

Baseball's New Frontier, by Fran Zimniuch & Branch Rickey III

Baseball's Power Shift, by Krister Swanson

Baseball Saved Us by Ken Mochizuki

Beyond the Scoreboard, by Rick Horrow & Karla Swatek

Built to Last, by Jim Collins & Jerry I. Porras

Clemente, by Kal Wagenheim & Wifrid Sheed

Clemente, by the Clemente Family

Circling the bases, by Andrew Zimbalist

Diamond Dollars, by Vince Gennaro

Dias de Sacrificio, Gloria y Esperanza, by Félix Feliz

Don't Wait for the Next War, by Wesley K. Clark

Dollar Sign on the Muscle, by Kevin Kerrane

Everything is Obvious, by Duncan J. Watts

Expanding the Strike Zone: Baseball in the Age of Free Agency, by Daniel A. Gilbert

Feewding the Monster: How money, smarts, and nerve took a team to the top, by Seth Mnookin

Field of Schemes, by Neil deMause & Joanna Cagan

Homenaje al Número 21: Roberto Clemente Walker, by Edwin Vázquez

How You Play the Game, by Jerry Colangelo & Len Sherman

In Pursuit of Pennants, by Mark L. Armour & Daniel R. Levitt

Inside Pitch and More, by Gene A. Budig

In the Best Interests of Baseball, by Andrew Zimbalist

Las Estrellas Orientales: Cómo el béisbol cambió el pueblo dominicano de San Pedro de Macorís, by Mark Kurlansky

May the Best Team Win, by Andrew Zimbalist & Bob Costas

Molina: The story of the Father Who Raised an Unlikely Baseball Dynasty, by Bengie Molina con Joan Ryan

Naked Economics, by Charles Wheelan

Perfectly Legal, by David Cay Johnston

Pirates 1960 Yearbook, by the Pittsburgh Baseball Club

Players, by Mathew Futterman

Public Dollars, Private Stadiums, by Kevin J. Delaney & Rick Eckstein

Regulating the National Pastime, by Jerold J. Duquette

Revolutionary Wealth, by Alvin & Heidi Toffler

Scorecasting, by Tobias J. Moskowitz & L. Jon Wertheim

Speaking of Success, by Ken Blanchard, Jack Canfield, Gary Parks

Sports Analytics, by Benjamin C. Alamar

Sports in America, by James A. Michener

Stadium Games, by Jay Weiner

The American Diamond, by Branch Rickey

The business of Sports, by Scott R. Rosnier & Kenneth L. Shropshire

The Cardinals Way, by Howard Megdal

The Game, by Jon Pessah

The Grind, by Barry Svrluga

The Next Convergence, by Michael Spence

The Power of Negative Thinking, by Bob Knight

The Sabermetric Revolution, by Benjamin Baumer & Andrew Zimbalist

There's no such thing as Business Ethics, by John C. Maxwell & Steven R. Covey

Who Owns the Future, by Jaron Lanier

The Author

*I*n 1972, at age sixteen emigrated from Puerto Rico to Chicago. He played baseball at Roberto Clemente Community Academy, but despite his flawless third base performance, he dropped-out high school and obtained a job with Florsheim Shoe Company. In June 1976, he took upon the U.S. Army's Combat Medical occupation. Alternating duty between combat field units, hospitals and clinics, cross-cultural and gender advisory at brigade level, Army Reserve Components military advisory, formal instruction of junior enlisted and officers, culminating a brilliant career in test and evaluation of medical technologies.

He served in the 4th Infantry at Fort Carson; 9th Infantry at Fort Lewis; 25th Infantry at Schofield Barracks; 1st and 2nd US Army Reserve Components Groups at Fort Buchanan; US Army Medical Activity at Panama; Madigan Army Medical Center at Fort Lewis; Brooke Army Medical Center at Fort Sam Houston; 21st Evacuation Hospital at Saudi Arabia; and Combat Medical Division, Military Medical Science Division, and Army Medical Department Board at Fort Sam Houston.

While in the Army he completed a bachelor's degree in education from Southern Illinois University at Carbondale. After retirement in 2002 obtained a post-graduate degree in Upper-Level Business Management from Universidad Panamericana, Panama. Then he went to International University Panama and obtained a master's in business reengineering and TQM, and a Professorship certificate.

He retired in the rank of Master Sergeant, lives in the Tampa Bay area and his books sell in Amazon. Visit his blog: www.lordsereno.com

www.ingramcontent.com/pod-product-compliance
Lightning Source LLC
Chambersburg PA
CBHW031534040426
42445CB00010B/528